HERE'S THE THING

SELECTED INTERVIEWS, VOLUME 2

by

GREG JOHNSON

Counter-Currents Publishing Ltd.
San Francisco
2020

Copyright © 2020 by Greg Johnson
All rights reserved

Cover design by
Kevin I. Slaughter

Published in the United States by
COUNTER-CURRENTS PUBLISHING LTD.
P.O. Box 22638
San Francisco, CA 94122
USA
http://www.counter-currents.com/

ISBNs
Hardcover Edition: 978-1-64264-159-2
Paperback Edition: 978-1-64264-160-8
Electronic Edition: 978-1-64264-161-5

Contents

Preface ❖ iii

1. Decline of the West: Interview with Darryl Cooper ❖ 1

2. White Identity Politics: Interview with Tara McCarthy ❖ 48

3. From Metapolitics to Hegemony: Interview with Lana Lokteff ❖ 73

4. Destigmatizing Racism: A Conversation with Hugh MacDonald ❖ 96

5. Answering Sargon of Akkad: Interview with Millennial Woes ❖ 113

6. Answering Normie Questions: Interview with JM ❖ 134

7. Vanity, Pretentiousness, & Snobbery: A Conversation with Hugh MacDonald ❖ 160

8. Conversation with a Philosopher ❖ 181

9. Straight but Not Narrow Nationalism: Interview with Maureen O'Connor ❖ 205

10. What's Wrong With Modernity?: Interview with Liz Bruenig ❖ 208

Index ❖ 213

About the Author ❖ 222

Preface

This is my second volume of interviews. The first, *You Asked for It: Selected Interviews*, vol. 1 appeared from Counter-Currents in 2017. I knew that there would be future volumes, because when I first published my interviews and transcripts on the *Counter-Currents* webzine, they were quite popular.

Interviews tend to be wordier than written texts, but, paradoxically, they often *feel* shorter because they are more engaging. Being interviewed forces one to communicate complex ideas more directly. Every interview is addressed to a specific individual rather than to the world as a whole, but, again paradoxically, many people find it less engaging to be addressed as part of the general public than to "listen in" on other people's conversations.

In editing these transcripts, I have introduced paragraph and sentence breaks, dropped false starts, supplied missing conclusions, gotten rid of hosts of "sort of," "kind of," and "and so forth" locutions, and quietly corrected some mistakes. I eliminated chit-chat whenever doing so did not interrupt the flow of the conversation. Words attributed to others are not verbatim quotations but summaries of the gist of their ideas. It would, however, take a complete rewrite to transform these interviews into semblances of my written works, so the quality of the spoken word remains.

I want to thank the original interviewers: Darryl Cooper, Tara McCarthy, Lana Lokteff, Hugh MacDonald, Millennial Woes, JM, the anonymous philosopher, Maureen O'Connor, and Liz Bruenig. I also want to thank those who transcribed the first eight interviews, as well as Kevin Slaughter, who created the cover, and Scott Weisswald, Alex Graham, and James O'Meara, who helped bring this book to press.

This book is dedicated to Vera Gottfried, the little German.

November 27, 2020

Decline of the West

Interview with
Darryl Cooper*

Darryl Cooper: Hey everybody, this is Daryl Cooper. This is *Decline of the West* podcast episode six. I'm here with Greg Johnson, founder and editor of Counter-Currents Publishing. How are you doing Greg?

Greg Johnson: I'm fine. Thank you for having me on the show.

DC: Yeah, it's good to have you here. I'm glad to hear it. So, there is a lot of ground I want to cover with you today. And so out of respect for your time, I'm ready to jump right into this. So why don't you tell us a little bit about Counter-Currents Publishing and what it is you guys do, and I guess start there.

GJ: I founded Counter-Currents Publishing in 2010 with Michael Polignano, who was my business partner for the first three years of it. Counter-Currents was founded as a publishing house; we do print publishing—we publish books—and we also have a webzine. I call it *North American New Right*, but everyone calls it *Counter-Currents*.

The purpose of *Counter-Currents* is to provide a forum for writers who are broadly compatible with the project of creating a New Right in North America, and by a New Right I mean a metapolitical approach to changing politics. We wish to change people's ideas about identity and morality to lay the foundations for actual political change.

The political order we envision is ethno-nationalist. We want to create a white homeland in North America for people of Eu-

---

* This interview for Darryl Cooper's *Decline of the West* podcast was recorded in September of 2016. I thank Thanatos for the transcript.

ropean descent. And the reason for that is very simple. We don't think that multiculturalism is working out very well for white people. We look around the world, and in every white society, birth rates are below replacement.

There are many causes for this, but the principal cause, in our view, is that we've lost sovereign control of our homelands. There are no white societies that make the preservation of their people and our race as a whole a political priority. They're chasing other dreams instead. And that has instituted really alarming demographic trends.

Due to a culture of consumerism and selfishness, people are not reproducing. There are all kinds of economic and cultural incentives to not reproduce. There are also incentives to reproduce outside the race (miscegenation), and we're finding that our living spaces are being invaded by nonwhites who are highly fertile.

So we're losing control of our homelands, and we think that that has to be reversed both in Europe, where our race comes from, and also in the European colonial societies like the United States or Canada or Australia, New Zealand, or places in South America like Argentina or Uruguay, which are still largely of European descent.

DC: Okay. Thank you. That introduction is going to be pretty jarring to a lot of listeners. So this is going to lead straight into my first real question. And, this is going to serve as an introduction to the rest of the questions from you. So if you'll indulge me for a few minutes, it'll take me a minute to build up to, I just want to be very clear about where I'm going with this first question.

I've always been very fascinated with people who make a decision to split off from the mainstream when they very clearly have a choice to do otherwise. I love John Krakauer's books. For example, he wrote *Into Thin Air* about his experience climbing Mount Everest when a bunch of people in his group died up there, and he doesn't weigh himself down with the technical details about climbing. He doesn't wax aesthetic about the majesty of the mountain or the lovely views of the grand ambition of human achievement or any of that. He spends most of the book explaining in grinding detail what an utterly miserable experience the entire thing is; you have a headache, you're nauseous, you can't eat, you can't even enjoy it because the oxygen level's so brutal, and all these things. And he tries to get to the bottom of what kind of a person would do this to himself and why.

He wrote a book about Christopher McCandless, a smart upper middle-class kid who graduated from college because he felt that it was his duty to meet his parents' expectations up to that point for having raised him. But then he splits off and he wanders through the wastelands around the Salton Sea in the desert in Nevada, working his way up eventually to Alaska. And when he gets there, he abandons his car and burns the last of his money, and he goes off like the title of the book says, *Into the Wild*.

This kid ran into a lot of people on the way. He developed relationships. He had a profound impact on a lot of the people he met. So this was not some kid who lost his mind. He wasn't crazy in any sense of the word that would still retain its meaning. He knew exactly what he was doing, and this was a decision that he made.

So somebody like you is very interesting to me. You could play society's game if you wanted to. You've got your Ph.D. in philosophy. That speaks not only to your intellectual horsepower, which you know has never been incompatible with eccentricity. But more importantly it speaks to the fact that you know how to play the game. Showing up on time every day, the discipline of work, the being able to navigate a university environment for many years. That whole part of it.

Now today you run Counter-Currents Publishing, and I don't know how many books are out, but you're pretty prolific. So all of this speaks to the fact that you could have shut your mouth, maybe kept your social and political philosophy close to the vest, maybe venting on certain issues when you knew you were among like-minded friends, and so forth. You could have become a successful academic or writer. You could have done the bourgeois thing without bringing into your life the complications and the difficulties that you must have known the path that you chose was going to invite. The forces in our societies that are aligned against people like you are powerful and ubiquitous, and they know what they're doing.

I mentioned to you before we started recording that I'm going to be interviewing a black nationalist soon and a Right-wing Zionist settler from the area outside Hebron. I had to really think about whether I wanted to do this interview, because I knew that I could interview those other two guys with no problems. But I know that there's a good chance that just having a conversation with you is going to possibly make not only my own life more difficult in certain ways, but could even cascade down on to my family and people who know me, because that's how the forces that are aligned against people like you operate.

I apologize again for this long-winded introduction to this question, but I guess I wanted to make clear that this isn't the standard question that opens a lot of interviews like this, which is some form of why do you think what you think or how did you get to think this way. A lot of people think a lot of things, and when those thoughts are too psychologically or socially hazardous, most of us are pretty good about just stuffing them back down, so that we can get back to our lives.

I'm interested in the path that caused you to cross over that gulf. Were there were events or revelations or flashes of insight? I'm interested in the path that led you to decide that the drama implied by breaking your own society's most dangerous taboos were not going to be sufficient to deter you from this path. That it wasn't going to be enough for you to have an opinion, but that you had to act, and you even had to devote your life to something that you knew would invite not just incomprehension but real hostility and real hatred and social and professional consequences onto yourself. So can you talk about that a little bit?

GJ: I don't want to give myself too much credit. On the one hand, I've always been somewhat contrarian. When I was a high school student and even before that, when I was in my early teens, I was very interested in history and culture. A lot of it was art history, but also ancient history, archaeology, etc.

I was very interested in exotic cultures: Amerindian societies, Mesoamerican and South American Indian civilizations, Easter

Island, etc. Thor Heyerdahl was a great hero of mine when I was young. I think I read my first Thor Heyerdahl book when I was twelve years old. It was *Fatu Hiva*, and then I read *Aku-Aku* after that.

One of the things that I learned from the experiences of nonwhite peoples in Polynesia and also the Americas is just how fragile civilization is, and how civilizations that are very ancient in their roots and very powerful, can still be really brittle when encountering outside forces that are sufficiently ruthless and have certain technological and organizational advantages, and how a world can end. And these worlds ended over and over again. I was very impressed with the art of these people and saddened to see the destruction of their material civilization, and, of course, we know almost nothing about their actual beliefs, so their spiritual civilization was even more fragile. Things like that were very important to me.

I was a big Egyptophile when I was a kid and a teenager. I studied the history of Egypt. I used to know all the pharaohs of the major dynasties. I used to know all the Roman and Byzantine emperors and pretenders. My brain was a sponge for that kind of information.

Of course, the lessons recur over and over again about the fragility of civilization. So I had a strong sense that our own civilization is very fragile. Very beautiful things we created could be lost, potential creation and exploration could be nipped in the bud, if people didn't make the right decisions.

So I had a strong sense that civilization is very fragile. I also had a strong sense that we were making all the wrong decisions. I used to be a libertarian. I used to think that statism was the wrong choice. And, of course, if you look at Communism in the twentieth century, it's a very easy conclusion to draw.

DC: Sure.

GJ: I also had a sense that if people don't speak out about these problems when they're getting started or when they're in their earlier stages, it's very irresponsible, because as these problems progress over time, it gets harder and harder to correct them. If you're trying to get from point A to point B, and there's a 1% deviation in the course at the very beginning, well that's easy to correct after a few steps. But if you go hundreds of miles, suddenly it's very difficult to get to the target.

I always had a strong sense that initial decisions, fundamental principles, have long-term consequences, and if you don't get things right from the start, as time passes, it becomes harder and harder to correct things. And, therefore, farsighted people need to speak up; they need to be brave.

I was always less motivated than my peers by social approval. I don't know why that is. It has just always been the way that I am. When I was a teenager or even younger, people would try to talk to me about God, and I would get impatient because it sounded like they weren't making any sense. And I'd say I just don't believe this, I'm sorry. I knew there were social consequences for that, but when their eyes and mouths grew wide in shock, I am ashamed to say I found that a little bit satisfying. I enjoyed that effect. I didn't say things just for the effect, but it didn't bother me that I believe things that were out of step with the rest of humanity.

Okay, so flash forward to when I get my doctorate and go off into academia. At the time I would have been ripe for the picking, easily co-opted by the system. I worked a long time. I wrote and studied, and I had an excellent education. I could think and write rings around a lot of my peers. However, when I was coming out of my Ph.D. program, political correctness was already stifling in academia, and it's only gotten worse. I can't imagine being in that environment now.

I basically couldn't find a decent job anywhere. I knew silly females in graduate school who had just defended a dissertation prospectus about writing feminist interpretations of their three favorite movies. Something that's stupid and easy to do. A dissertation on how they feel as a woman about their three favorite movies. And these women would go off and get thirteen or fourteen job interviews for tenure-track jobs. That's how insane the system was around 2000 and 2001, when I started going on the job market. And it's only gotten worse since then.

So if the system had cared about co-opting me, I might be a tenured professor at some university churning out articles that might be read by seven to ten people. And books that might be bought by a few hundred libraries. And people might leaf through them a few hundred times, and a dozen people might read them cover to cover. And that's basically the life of an academic, where you do grindingly overly-detailed research that almost nobody reads and has almost no impact on the world.

And here's the sad and pathetic thing about it: I would have been absolutely delighted with that life. But it was denied me. The system didn't co-opt me, didn't give me all that security and comfort that I would be too afraid to lose. And it's not because I was outwardly politically incorrect, although I think these people could sense that I didn't want to play their little reindeer games. The main problem was just being pale and male. That was my main handicap. It had nothing to do with my thinking. They didn't want me for my mind, basically.

So I ended up having a short inglorious academic career, and by the time that I was out of academia and I had decided that I'm not going to torture myself trying to get back into a job surrounded by these people, I was very much into the White Nationalist scene, and I could see all kinds of ways that I could make it better. And so that's what I decided to do, and, as Pepe the Frog says, "It feels good, man." I write articles that are read by thousands or tens of thousands of people. Even things that I write on philosophers get read a lot. They get discussed a lot. I actually have an impact on the world that I could not have had if I had remained in academia.

One of the things that I've been talking about for the past few years is the army that I'm going to raise up. Is Greg Johnson building an army? The answer is yes. I'm building an army of NEETs. Building an army of people who are not in education, employment or training. They're basically people who went to college, got educations, racked up huge amounts of student debt. They're all white, of course. They racked up huge amounts of student debt, and then they ended up working full time or part time stocking shelves at Trader Joe's or Whole Foods or something like that, or as baristas. Because the Obama economy has no need for educated white people.

There was a *Breitbart* article, five or six years ago now, about how 25% of recent college graduates in the state of New Jersey were living with their parents. The system has stopped co-opting them too. So one of the things that's contributing massively, mightily, to the growth of the Alternative Right is that there are a lot of very smart young white people who don't have anything to lose, because they don't have a job, they don't have a mortgage, and they don't have a future anyway. There's nothing that the system can threaten to take away. And at the same time, they can envision toppling this system and replacing it with something better.

That's what the White Nationalist movement really is all about. We have a plausible explanation for why people who were told that they were tomorrow's leaders are now underemployed and deeply in debt. We also have plausible solutions for that. The Occupy Movement with its "progressive stack" and unfocused kvetching about banks and devotion to anti-racism, basically anti-whiteism, does not have an answer, so Occupy basically withered away.

But the Alternative Right as they call it, White Nationalism as I call it, is growing, and it's growing because we have a constituency. The constituency has not been co-opted by the system. In fact it's been alienated by the system, and they have plenty of time on their hands, plenty of motivation and access to the internet. Thus far, it's been largely an online movement, but now we're taking it offline into the 3D world, and a lot of the people who are showing up are tremendously impressive. So we're going to be a terror in the next ten or fifteen years. The world that we live in is going to change very rapidly. I do not think America as it exists today will exist in 2025.

DC: Something that you just said, definitely, it's something I've observed. I think maybe ten or fifteen or twenty years ago, a lot of the time when you would think of a White Nationalist, you're not necessarily thinking of a savory character. And I think there was probably some justice to that stereotype. But a lot of the people that I'm meeting now, who self-identify as Alt Right, like you said, are college-educated people who are well put-together, who carry themselves well, who often have families that are at a young age and who take care of them. It's definitely a different brand of people than the Venice Beach skinhead that I would have run into when I was a kid. I don't want to leave that theme of alienation that you were talking about right now, but we're going to get into that in a little bit. I kind of have that ear-marked.

There's one question I wanted to ask about your introduction. I came around to the idea that civilizations are fragile a little bit differently than you did, although I assume there's probably some intersection. I, like a lot of high-school boys, read Nietzsche a lot, and in my early twenties, I got to Oswald Spengler, and I love Spengler. I love Spengler today. I don't adopt his ideology as whole cloth as I used to, but I still love him for the gift that he gave me at the time.

Spengler famously, or maybe infamously in White Nationalist circles, prioritized culture over race. And in the 1930s, he was openly critical of the mere zoology as he called it of the National Socialists. And when he did talk about race, it was clear that the concept for him was rooted in metaphysics rather than just a sort of simple materialist biology.

Who are some of the thinkers that have influenced your views on race, and is your social and political philosophy rooted in a metaphysical conception of race or something closer to home? Like maybe the sociological perspective that might've flowed from somebody like Robert Putnam, maybe if he'd had the courage to follow through his ideas to their conclusion. You talked about the fragility of civilization, but what was the thing that knotted together the idea of race and civilization for you? Because there's a lot of people today, at least in the United States and Europe for sure, who would not necessarily force that connection.

GJ: I came upon Spengler somewhat later than you. It was in graduate school when I read *Decline of the West*. It's a magnificent book, a truly magnificent work of the imagination, a magnificent synthesis, and a very useful heuristic. A lot of it doesn't ring true. You can quibble with a lot of his facts, and I think his underlying relativism is too extreme. I don't believe that it's meaningful to talk about different mathematics in different civilizations. I don't think that stands the test of philosophical argument. That said, it's a brilliant heuristic.

It's essentially a kind of Epicurean account of the rise and fall of civilization. It is a cyclical view of history, but it's not Traditionalist but Epicurean in inspiration. The thinker who is closest to my mind, the thinker whom I find to be one of the most adequate as well as pregnant with new possibilities in the philosophy of history and culture, is Giambattista Vico. I love Vico. He was a great reactionary. There's an essay by Steven Holmes, "The Permanent Structure of Antiliberal Thought." It's basically a description of Vico. He doesn't make that clear, but Vico is the paradigm of the Enlightenment and post-Enlightenment critic of modernity and liberalism. I see Spengler as fitting into that tradition as well. Spengler was deeply influenced by Nietzsche, and I love Nietzsche too. But that's just bibliographical.

How does race figure into it? Spengler was just wrong about race because he thought that Franz Boas was telling the truth about race. He thought that Boas' studies that claim that people's heads changed when they moved to the New World and were in a different culture or a cultural environment or landscape refuted the idea that that race is mutable only by biological evolution. But we know now that Boas was making it up, that it was fraudulent, that it's not true. So if Spengler were around today, he might not hold the same view.

Spengler was part Jewish, and therefore he also had a personal motivation to be opposed to the kind of racial purist attitudes that were floating around in Germany in the interwar period, and certainly in the Third Reich. But those are questions I'd like to set aside.

My eyes glaze over and I get very uncomfortable when people talk about metaphysical notions of race. When Evola talks about race in different senses of the word, that's the weakest thing in his work. Race is simply a biological concept. That's all it is. If you want to talk about character types and the like, that's a separate issue. But race is a biological concept, and it's only a biological concept.

If people start talking about metaphysical notions of race,

they're either trying to bootleg in some kind of dualistic metaphysics, or they are confusing race with other categories that are perfectly legitimate and useful like the study of different character types or soul types, as in the Platonic psychology of reason, spirit, and desire, which allows you to talk about different types of men: the desire-driven man, the rational man, and the honor-driven man. Or the psychology of the temperaments and humors. All of these are perfectly legitimate. I just don't want to call them race. I just want to reserve that term for biology.

In terms of my own thinking about race, I was always deeply aware of it, because I was so fascinated with exotic peoples when I was a kid. My parents subscribed to *National Geographic*, and their friends had stacks of old ones in their basements from their kids, and they'd give them to me. I was just fascinated with physical anthropology and cultural anthropology from a very early age.

I was sort of a connoisseur, just on the surface, of different racial types. I could look at aborigines or Papuans or other peoples like that, and at a glance I could pretty much classify them in terms of racial and subracial types. I didn't have any negative attitudes towards other races because I grew up in an almost entirely white environment. My attitude towards them was fascination. I still have lots of books on my shelves about Amerindians, the Far East, Polynesia, and so forth. So it is both an old and an abiding interest to me.

Thus I never bought the idea that race was somehow a social construct or it's all culture. It took me years to understand where that was even coming from. It's basically a metaphysical posit of egalitarianism. They have a project of making everybody the same, and therefore they have to posit that the main stumbling block in the path of that, biological race, can somehow be ignored. And it's as simple as that. They constantly talk about deconstructing our concepts. We need to deconstruct their concepts. They constantly talk about how our concepts are just creations of our power drives and our agendas. Well, they're tipping their hand about their own ideas as well.

I've always been a person who's motivated by the truth, and I've changed my views on a lot of things very radically over time because I just found that certain arguments were better than others. I've always found the idea that systems of ideas are just expressions of their time and place or just ideologies, tools of domination, and so forth to be a tell. If people say that, chances are they practice what they preach. Their ideas are often just tools, and they're dishonest.

I took me a long time to come around to that because I've always been so naïve. I would think maybe I just need to analyze Foucault a little bit more, and then it'll make sense. Perhaps the problem lies in me. It took me many years before I finally just got to the point of declaring that certain systems of ideas are just nonsense, carefully constructed to serve a particular agenda. And they have to be deconstructed as that.

But I've never bought the race is a social construct stuff from the beginning. And once I got out into the world and started interacting with people instead of living in a completely white bubble, I started noticing that racial differences are not just exotic and interesting, but they're also absolutely crucial for determining people's likely behaviors, likely level of performance, likely level of civilization, likelihood of civilizational conflict and decline, and so forth. So it wasn't a great leap for me to become a race realist. I was a race realist for a long time before I actually decided, "Screw multiculturalism"; screw these forms of liberalism that I was clinging to. We simply must have homogeneous societies. We need to change the demographic composition and trends of our societies if we want to survive.

I've always been worried about demographics. It was always in the background, nagging and gnawing at me, even as I was holding onto universalistic political ideas like libertarianism or classical liberalism or conservatism. I worried that if our population is replaced by dumber people, none of this is going to work. And at a certain point, that nagging little voice in the back of my head got louder and louder, and finally I thought that I just had to change my political paradigm. We can't afford to play these little games anymore.

There was a time when I was a post-libertarian conservative trying to figure out ways of squaring the circle and maintaining a sensible, functional society in an increasingly multicultural environment. And when you just look at the trends, after a while you have to say: "No, it's not going to work."

For Republican conservative types, the last refuge before full-on White Nationalism is assimilationism. But even if we could assimilate all these people who are coming in, we're not even *trying*. They're assimilating us one taco at a time. And until such time as we start trying to assimilate these people, you need to stand up and say, "Halt! We can't have any more of this invasion."

I had so many conservative friends who would run screaming from the room when I would wag my finger at them and say, "If you really believe in assimilation, and we're not assimilating, you've got to blow the whistle and halt immigration." But no, they wanted to marry some girl from the Philippines. They always had some private reservations, or they were involved in globalized businesses, and it was a good for their balance. They were invested in undermining wages in America, for instance.

Long after I was a race realist, and long after I worried about demographic change, I finally got to the point of just saying that a universalistic conservative political ideology is just a sucker's proposition. Game theory helped on this. I was aware for a long time that if you have an environment where everyone's playing by individualist rules, and you come in working as a team, you have a systematic advantage. You demand that the individualists always give you a fair shake when they have something that you want. And when individualists come to you for some favor you can dispense, you duplicitously pretend like you're giving them a fair shake, and then you hand it off to your cousin and pretend that he's just the best guy for the job.

Well, we've been importing a lot of people like that into our society, and it's being hollowed out and taken over by these "parasite tribes," as John Robb likes to call them. But you can only hack individualist white society, you can only hollow it out so far, until it's like an image in *Atlas Shrugged* that always affected me, of a great tree that stood for hundreds of years and then came crashing down in a storm, and everyone was shocked to find that it was hollowed out and empty inside. It was just a shell.

That's what's happening to us. We have this fantastically powerful society, with great cities and industries, but it's being hollowed out. The people who built it are being replaced by other kinds of people who could never have built it and can never sustain it. And the people who built and sustained it, our ethnic group, is being constantly attacked. We're constantly off balance. We're constantly in retreat. We're slated for replacement. Our enemies gloat about our demographic decline. But there's going to come a point when we have a war or an economic crisis, and we will find that the resources of civility that got us through the Great Depression will not be there anymore. Eventually when this system is stress tested, parts are going to start flying off. It's just going to collapse.

We need to basically call a halt to this. It's not working. We need to move back to a society that is normatively European rather than multicultural, and that is ethnically European. The demographic decline of whites in America has been going on since 1965. In 1965, we were a 90% white society. Everything was normatively white, meaning that all the nonwhite groups were required to live up to white social and legal norms. That exercised and important pressure on them to make them more bearable to be around.

But the normative whiteness of our society has been thrown out, and the borders have been opened, and the founding white population is maybe 60% now. In many states, white children are a minority in kindergarten and first grade. That's the future in store for us. A lot of white people are aware of that, and they feel hopeless. They feel like our people do not have a future on this continent anymore. Indeed, if present trends continue, we don't.

I think that the solution to that begins with the realization that it took fifty years to get this into this horrible mess. And it might take fifty years to get us out. As a practicable political proposal, let's return to *status quo* 1965, and let's do it in fifty years. Let's halt immigration from the nonwhite world, and let's create incentives for these people to emigrate rather than immigrate. And in fifty years, the older members of those communities will have died of old age, and the younger ones who are reproducing will have emigrated, and we could go back to *status quo* 1965. Hell, I'd like to go further than that. And in 2065, when I'm dead and gone, I hope people will move the goalposts further.

But what matters is that it's a totally feasible plan. You just have to change the basic incentive structures and laws that have caused our demographic decline. And then you have to wait.

It's a perfectly fair proposal. Whites have accepted that deal. We've accepted living in a system where our kind has no future. It's perfectly fair for us to say we're changing the rules now. Now nonwhites have no future in this society, and I'm not using "no future" as a military or mafia euphemism for murder. I'm simply saying that the nonwhite population will decline to the point where it's negligible or non-existent for post-1965 groups.

There's no reason to have any of them here. They have homelands all over the globe to which they can return. But we have only one homeland, and we're losing it. Blacks and a few Hispanics and Amerindians have a claim to being here. We can deal with that later.

DC: I am getting the feeling, Greg, that you must have missed a Jon Stewart's address to the nation. You didn't get the message. This isn't your country. It never was. Come on, man.

GJ: Yeah, I missed that address to the nation.

DC: Didn't make an impact, maybe?

GJ: It didn't make an impact. But seriously, the gloating our enemies are constantly engaged in: as someone once said, they're partying today like it's 2043, like we're already a minority. And that is starting to spook the horses. It is starting to wake up ordinary white people. We're in a weird situation. And we have to ask ourselves: "What's the upside of sharing a continent and a political system with people who obviously hate us as a group?"

DC: I think I can understand why Leftists are into all this stuff. That's fine. I don't really care, because they're my enemy, and I don't really care what they think. But you're talking about conservatives, Republicans, and maybe even people who are very critical of some of the cultural Marxist ideology, yet who will react with real horror or hostility, as if you've said something really terrible, when you bring up even cutting off immigration, forget about White Nationalism or something like that.

And these will very often be people who are in full support of a Jewish ethnostate in Israel. If the Japanese were going to maintain a Japanese supermajority, they wouldn't think anything of that. But they think very differently when it comes to their own country and their own people. I think that part of it is educational brainwashing. There's definitely been a Leftist push in that direction. But I also think that the reason people are probably susceptible to it on the American Right has a lot to do with Christianity, and not just the turn the other cheek and love your neighbor kind of thing.

There's this idea in Christianity that Jesus has come to call out the people from among the nations. Come out, leave behind the old rivalries of blood and soil and all those things and join a community of the spirit. Or join a community, in a more secular way, that's based on a common assent to a set of ideas. And as long as you believe in these things and are part of this consensus, then you're a part of our people.

I can understand why people are attracted to that idea, because I think that humans have throughout history had this tendency to seek larger scale social formations. We go from band societies to tribes. We go from tribes to super tribes. We go from super tribes to chiefdoms to states to what we have now. And I understand how people can be attracted to that.

When the Left overreaches, as it has recently, people are still willing to come back to the ideas that you're talking about, or at least come back to the ideas that somebody like Donald Trump is talking about. They think of race as like a backup power system. They think it's a beautiful thing to have this community of the spirit or community of consensus. But they keep this backup power system in case that doesn't work out.

And over the last several years when the Left has been partying like it's 2043, with the rise of Black Lives Matter and what happened at the Donald Trump rally in San Jose, where people were burning American flags and attacking women and children purely because they are white Trump supporters, they start to realize that civic nationalism may be a beautiful idea, but if other people aren't playing that game, then clearly it's not going to work out very well.

I'm actually okay with being in this society as an individual, and we all make our own choices. But it's something that you alluded to earlier with game theory: That doesn't work when there are alliances within society that aren't operating that way. I think there's a reason that in liberal societies, we're very suspicious of secret societies. Because we know on some deep level, even if it doesn't get spoken about outwardly, that if you have coalitions within the society and that sort of nepotism, then the whole thing will break down, because it just doesn't work unless everybody's on board. As soon as people start to favor one another based on some identity that is smaller than the larger whole that we're all trying to participate in, then it all just breaks down, because as soon as one group cheats, everybody has to. Otherwise you're just going to get run over. So I understand the appeal of it on some level, the aesthetic appeal or whatever you want to call it. But I think you're probably right.

A lot of these people who talk about the Trump movement and the rise of the Alt Right being the result of decades of Republican rhetoric are completely insane. I think that the recent rise on the Right is entirely due to overreach from the Left. And is that the way you see it? Sounds like you do.

GJ: Of course. The people who can't distinguish us from Mitt Romney Republicans are idiots. They're on autopilot. Basically they're just Marxist ideologues on autopilot. And they come up with the most amazing bullshit. The stuff that Marxists say would be really quite entertaining if it didn't have any influence and wasn't contributing to driving society over a cliff, which it is.

The fact is that Republicans and especially religious conservatives are actually the most pious believers in universalism and anti-racism. I've said this many times: The Christian creationist who doesn't believe in evolution at all is more capable of believing in racial egalitarianism and actually practicing racial egalitarianism than the white liberal who believes in evolution but just thinks it somehow stopped at the brain, that brains are all somehow fluid and mutable and re-programmable culturally. And if we just get the incentives and the education and the uplift schemes and the rhetoric right, we can make all these people in the ghetto hike up their pants and turn their baseball caps around the right way and start being stockbrokers and concert violinists. They really do think that.

But liberals are 95% in agreement with us in terms of human biodiversity, whereas the creationist is 0% in agreement. They really do believe in magic. And that's what you have to believe to think that multiculturalism can work. You have to believe in "magic dirt," as people like to say. These Mexicans, as soon as they step over onto the magic dirt of America, are going to start becoming like us. They're going to suddenly become members of and willing participants in a high-trust Northern European style society. And it's magic, because we're not even going to *try* to assimilate them or pressure them into adopting our way of life. They're just going to do it spontaneously, because it's magic. That's patently silly.

But if you believe that God created the world out of nothing and species didn't evolve, you believe in wholesale magic. Creation is magic on the wholesale level. I always find it very amusing when Christians say they believe God created the world out of nothing but don't believe in the real presence of God in the Eucharist. That sounds fishy to them. That's too magical for their tastes. But be real. If you believe in magic wholesale, you can believe anything, really.

There's a great satisfaction for white people in believing in communities that are entirely spiritual. It has a kind of sublimity to it. It makes us feel very big and powerful to avow these things, precisely because it's not in accordance with what we see in reality. It makes us feel all the bigger for repeating these views and trying to live by them, because it causes suffering, and suffering ennobles us.

DC: It takes faith, right?

GJ: It takes faith, and it requires suffering. And we feel like we're ennobling ourselves through it. And there's a deep truth to the idea that there's something noble about people who are willing to suffer for ideals. But they have to be true and right ideals.

I'm a cultural idealist. I don't believe in cultural materialism. I believe that the origin of civilization, the origin of history, is the willingness of people to suffer and die for things that aren't real. That's how we get this world of art and literature and so on.

But it really only works when it's just us playing this game. We're so easily exploited by outsiders, who come in and they see this tendency towards idealism and this willingness to suffer and this feeling like we're really big people by undertaking impossible tasks.

There's a wonderful collection of essays on pathological altruism co-edited by Barbara Oakley and three others.[1] She's written a number of other books including *Cold-Blooded Kindness*, which is an absolutely fascinating book.[2] It's very well written. It's also fortified with lots of empirical studies. She's one of these writers like Malcolm Gladwell who writes in a very vivid, popular way, and yet she's bringing to bear really hard science. Basically it's a study of codependency and codependent enablers.

When I read that book, I thought, "Oh my God, it's me," because I have a tendency to enable people. And when I enable them, it makes me feel big and powerful. But I realized that I was not helping people. I was enabling them to stay in jobs and living situations and maintain habits that were bad for them, because it made me feel good about myself.

There's an immediate application of this codependent enabling model to pet hoarders. These people feel really good about themselves and powerful by having large numbers of animals around. But the animals are suffering. They have too many ani-

---

[1] Barbara Oakley, Ariel Knafo, Guruprasad Madhavan, and David Sloan Wilson, eds., *Pathological Altruism* (New York: Oxford University Press, 2012).

[2] Barbara Oakley, *Cold-Blooded Kindness: Neuroquirks of a Codependent Killer, or Just Give Me a Shot at Loving You, Dear, and Other Reflections on Helping That Hurts* (Buffalo, N.Y.: Prometheus, 2011).

mals to take care of. The animals are filthy and miserable and sick and suffering. Yet the pet hoarder feels very big and powerful and good.

I think a lot of liberal psychology towards nonwhite immigrants is basically this kind of pet-hoarding ego trip. They gain a sense of efficacy and bigness by enabling these people to live in their societies. And the very fact that other people around them are discomforted by this and say this isn't good adds to the ego trip. They feel they're superior to those white people because they're willing to suffer more. These peace- and love-mongers are on total ego trips. And yet at the same time, they think of themselves as altruistic. They present themselves as altruistic and yet they're harming everybody in their relationships.

I would say this explains 95% of the behavior of white liberals towards nonwhites. Especially people who make excuses for nonwhite immigration into white societies and the persistence of pathological nonwhite behavior patterns. They're giving themselves little dopamine highs by feeling big and powerful and superior to those white people who aren't with the program. They are loving and taking care of these people who are here until the societies are overrun and destroyed, just like the pet hoarder's house is overrun and destroyed by cats. I know that psychology is very seductive because it seduced me. It's shameful. I've harmed people while being on this grand ego trip.

But part of the genesis of civilization is the willingness of people to not be practical. To even risk death for ideas. We have to realize that this is one of our strengths. It has just been perverted. Something very perverse and sick has been grafted onto it, and we need to be able to understand what's good at root and then what's pathological in branch. Then we need to lop off those sickly branches and return our society to health.

DC: Yeah. The codependency angle is very interesting because as I mentioned to you, I've been talking to a black nationalist too. And maybe you wouldn't be surprised how much alike you guys sound in certain ways. I think the general public gets this idea that the White Nationalist movement is just simply, "We don't like those people. We don't want them here." But the black nationalist that I've been talking to, he sort of echoes what you're saying, that this is not good for us either. Like the liberal social psychology professor at NYU, Jonathan Haidt. I don't know if you've met him or heard of him. But he often repeats this phrase, "Diversity is divisive," and it's kind of a tautology.

Yet when I've repeated that tautology to people, they have a Pavlovian negative response to it. Like they don't want to hear it. And the sentiment kind of echoes the conclusions of the sociologist Robert Putnam. He said the same thing. And when he discovered that, he was very reluctant to even release it, because he's a very progressive sociology professor, and he was dismayed by what he found. But he's an honest and earnest scholar. So he put it out there, and he's made the same point.

You talk a little bit about alienation and anxiety and the hit that social trust seems to take from living in a diverse multicultural society. And there are going to be a lot of people listening to this, and a lot of people who are the type of people we've been talking about on the Right, Republicans and even Donald Trump voters who want to build the wall. They are very familiar with that feeling of alienation and anxiety.

But they are wearing that same Pavlovian shock collar that I just mentioned. So they're pretty well-conditioned to attribute those feelings to anything other than diversity or multiculturalism. So what would you say to some of those people? What case would you make to those people to get them past that conditioning to consider what you would say are the real roots of these feelings? That's a central challenge that the White Nationalist movement faces at this point.

GJ: I think the main problem is that these people are being lied to by conservative intellectuals and opinion leaders, who are just liars about this issue: the people who say the problem with Detroit is all those Democrats. I mock these people all the time. "I got off the train in the wrong neighborhood, and I was terrified. I was surrounded by all these Democrats. I was afraid they were going to beat me up and pick my pocket. So I got back on the train to try to get away from all those Democrats. These liberal Democrats are really scary people." They know better than that, and you just have to rub their noses in it. The problem with Detroit is not liberal Democrats. Somehow Seattle, which is run by liberal Democrats, is not like Detroit, which is run by liberal Democrats.

The key is to just be real with normies and to give them permission to be real. There is no plausible account of the structure of the human amygdala that says that people are wired to feel fear around liberal Democrats, but there's a very plausible account about how the brain is structured that shows that it's natural, normal, and right for people to feel fear and anxiety around people of different races. That's just the way people are. It starts very early, practically as soon as we can focus our eyes. So it's before social conditioning. We respond favorably to people who look like us or are genetically similar, and we respond disfavorably to people who are genetically different. That's just how we're wired, and that's one of the factors that determine how comfortable we are in a social situation.

Now there are other factors as well. You might be with a black man who speaks standard English, and if you can communicate well with him, you feel a lot more comfortable with him than if he speaks with a heavy accent or he's babbling some unintelligible language. And if he's babbling loudly and angrily, and showing the whites of his eyes, then you feel really frightened. So there are social factors as well.

But you know, we're not just importing different races, we're importing different races and hundreds of different ethnic groups at the same time. And that just adds to it. There are only so many races in the world, and we don't have Bushmen from Africa or Australian aborigines coming here. Only a few racial groups are actually coming here, and if it were just that simple it would be less problematic. But people from hundreds of different cultures are coming into the United States. There are shops in New York City that sell publications in hundreds of different languages.

DC: They're running into this issue in Europe right now because they say, "Oh, we're taking Muslim refugees." And in a lot of these refugee neighborhoods and camps, they're starting to find out that you can't just say that they're "Muslim" refugees, because a lot of these people don't identify with one another at all. So they're having gang wars between different groups. And I think we do tend to clump peoples together like that.

GJ: There is a sense of Muslim brotherhood. But it's pretty thin if you look at the kind of absolute savagery that is going on in civil wars in the Muslim world right now.

DC: There's an Arab proverb that's pretty famous: "Me against my brother, and my brother and I against my cousin, and my brother and my cousin and I against the world, or against the stranger." I think there is an aspect to identity that always identifies against an other. I don't think that if everybody were the same in the world that would ever occur to anybody to think of themselves as white or black or anything like that. But I really don't know if identity necessarily can exist without the presence of an other.

I want to get into a few other questions. Doing my research for this interview, I didn't read too deeply into your views on capitalism and liberal democracy, but I got the impression that you're probably at least as critical of those things as I am, and I'm very critical of both of them. So, what role do they play in creating and sustaining the atomization of our societies relative to diversity and multiculturalism, or in your view, can these things really even be teased out from one another?

GJ: Yeah, there's a lot there. Let me just tell you what I think is right, and then we can get to capitalism and liberal democracy. I am a kind of classical republican, meaning this: I think that the best kind of society was the one outlined, say, in Aristotle's *Politics* where you have a large middle class or large number of people who have property and who are self-employed. So I believe in private property, widely distributed, as a condition of liberty. I think liberty is an important value. It's not the most important value, but it is an important social value. And I think that private property widely distributed is one of the conditions of liberty.

I think that we need a mixed regime, *à la* Aristotle, where you've got a monarchical element, an aristocratic element, and a popular element, and those things all have roles to play. The monarchical figure is necessary because especially in times of emergency, you need somebody who brings discussion and deliberation to a close and acts

DC: Sovereignty principle, Schmitt and so forth.

GJ: Yes. You need a decider and an actor who takes responsibility. Schmitt points out that what underlies liberal democracy is the hope that we can always just keep talking. Then we'll never have to stop talking and make decisions and take responsibility for those decisions and force people to go along with them. So you need the monarchical principle, the one guy who decides and takes the consequences.

The aristocratic principle is important because people aren't equal, and all of us want to be governed by people who are better than average. It just makes sense. If you get the choice of being governed by average people, below-average people, or above-average people, obviously you want to be governed by above-average people, because you get better results that way. So you need a way of making sure that positions of responsibility go into the hands of people who are wiser and more honest and public-spirited than average.

But if you just have aristocracy, you have the danger that these people are going to start governing for their own class interests. Therefore, you need the rest of the populace to play some kind of role in checking the tendency of monarchical figures or aristocratic groups to be corrupt. So you've got to have all three forms of government checking and balancing one another.

I think private property is one of the important sources of liberty. However, unregulated capitalism, especially financial capitalism, has a tendency towards the concentration of power and wealth in the hands of a few. And you do not want to be ruled by people who are simply richer than average. That's one of the bad forms of government. You want to be ruled by people who are wiser than average and responsive to the general public. That's how you get to the common good as opposed to just basically a society that's factional.

So there's a role for private property. There's a role for private enterprise, but there's also a necessity of regulating these things whenever they conflict with the common good. It's perfectly fine to have markets. However, as soon as you start on the road to globalization, you start undermining polities, undermining communities, introducing factionalism, and therefore you need economic protectionism at the very least to preserve sovereignty.

You don't want some fool who thinks foreign policy is really expensive and difficult to outsource it to a foreign country. That would be insane. You've got to at least protect certain industries that are connected with your national sovereignty.

As for liberalism, it is simply a political compromise that became an ideology and a metaphysics. Liberalism came about after the Reformation to put an end to the wars between Catholics and Protestants. We decided that peace is more important than arguing and fighting about the differences between Christian sects.

That's all well and good, but now it's been turned into a metaphysics. Today people concerned about maintaining liberalism argue for relativism just because they're terrified that if somebody believes that something is true and good, they'll reach for a club and bash their neighbor's head in. That's folly, because you can't found a workable society on relativism, and having a workable society is more important than the liberty of everybody's opinion.

DC: Yeah. I run into this type of conversation all the time, and I've run into it recently when Donald Trump gave his talk about maternity care and maternity leave. I got into a debate on Twitter about it with a libertarian with a talk show. And all he would say is "It's economically inefficient." I just kept repeating, I don't give a shit. I don't care. The fact we have working, intelligent, productive mothers who don't feel like they have the capability to take time off to have children, or at least they don't have time or the resources to do it until they're farther along, maybe in their late thirties or so. And we have to fix that somehow. One way or another. And maybe this doesn't work. Maybe we have to try something else. But we have to try something. And if it's economically efficient, I don't care. We've got to do something and run with it.

GJ: Economic efficiency is a dubious value.

DC: It's an idol to these people. And I almost feel like it's an idol to a lot of the people on the standard Right, cuckservative types. Because freedom and liberty are fine; they're great. But it's a purely negative value. Freedom to do what? Liberty for what? And nobody really has an answer to that. So they settle on liberty to make money, liberty to have property. I guess that's all they can offer you. Then they're surprised when something like the Alt Right is actually giving people a positive project, whatever people may think about it. Some people think it's pathological. You have a group of people who are coming out of the Right, which has, in my opinion, been completely emptied of any type of positive idea or project. And now people are being offered something, and they're surprised that it appeals to people. And I don't understand their confusion, to be honest with you.

GJ: Part of it is just fear. There's this article by Judith Shklar called "The Liberalism of Fear." That's basically what drives liberalism. It's fear of conflict, fear of oppression, and so forth. Fear of real debates about values. But everybody wants more stuff. That's a low, base set of motives. But everybody shares it. Therefore we can found society on a least common denominator, the pursuit of wealth.

DC: Sure. Yeah. I think anything that everybody shares is not really worth attaining to me. You'll hear this from conservatives all the time, when they're pushing the war in Iraq to build democracy. They'll say, you go to Iraq, you go to Afghanistan, and people everywhere just want to raise their families in peace and make a living. And my response is those are not human values. Every mammal wants to do that. That's what every cow wants to do. Any mammal wants to raise its family in peace and make a living. There's nothing positive there that's interesting at all. I think it's very vapid.

GJ: It is vapid. And of course, in all these societies, this peaceful, mammalian behavior—the kind of behavior that Plato describes in the *Republic* as the city of pigs, where everyone's just basically living in some kind of vegetarian matriarchy and are only concerned with comfort and security—disappears very quickly when men grow up and start fighting with one another over things that aren't real, like honor. Like their self-image. That's what drives history. That's the beginning of history for Hegel. These fierce-looking bearded Muslim types, that bow-tied conservatives claim "just wanna have fun," don't just wanna have fun. They wanna have fights. That's true of all men, even Western men. But it doesn't fit in with the whole desire-based model of liberal capital consumerist society. It's a false understanding of man.

Plato talks about this in the *Republic*, and I always come back to it. I think it's a fully adequate psychology, infinitely superior to Freud. Plato talks about how the soul has three parts. There's reason, spirit, and desire. Spirit basically has to do with honor and one's love of one's own, as well as the capacity to love things that aren't real, to be passionate about ideals, culture, and so forth. It's the root of patriotism, the root of fanaticism, etc.

And when you look at the early modern philosophers, the people who created the modern mind, who wired us up—people like Hobbes, Locke, and Hume—they're aware that man has this spirited part of the soul, and they're even willing to exploit it to some extent. But they are very concerned to bottle it up. The modern bourgeois conception of man is basically a desire-driven creature who uses reason as an instrument. Hobbes says reason is to the desires as scouts and spies. Reason goes out there as scouts and spies to get the stuff that satisfies the desires. It's purely instrumental. That's modern man. He's a desire-driven creature who has the faculty of instrumental reason, technology, science. He's a very clever mammal.

Those things that cause men to fight as opposed to consume and produce, well, that's "pride and vainglory." Those have to be bottled up. Locke wants to secure the world for the people he describes as "industrious and rational." "Industrious" meaning desire-driven and "rational" meaning using their reason to satisfy their desires. And who are the great enemies of the industrious and the rational? The "contentious and quarrelsome." The spirited man. We have been so bamboozled by these people.

Fast-forward to Freud. Freud has no concept of honor. The closest thing you get to honor in Freud is narcissism. And this is the standard chick attitude about men. "Oh, he's so egotistical. Oh, would you put aside your silly ego? Oh, you're just narcissistic. You should feel ashamed of that." We don't have a positive concept of honor. Yet that middle part of the soul, *thumos*, is the driving force of history. And we've been taught not to even understand what that is.

DC: I feel that probably goes a long way toward explaining the war that Northern American English have been making on the Scots-Irish in the South for a long time, arguably up to today. I read something similar in the last couple of years. Steven Pinker, in his book *Better Angels of our Nature*, states what you're saying very explicitly. He says honor is a bad thing. We need to get rid of the idea of honor, rid of the idea of patriotism, all of these things.

You have the industrious, rational North making war on the Scots-Irish in the South. And when you look at the core of Donald Trump's support today, these are the people that Kevin McCarthy is denouncing in the *National Review*, saying that they need to die off, that these communities need to go. There's definitely a real hostility there.

I want to ask you a little bit about United States specifically. Your most recent post on *Counter-Currents* was a remembrance of Francis Parker Yockey, who's best-known for his first book *Imperium*, and as a title that implies he advocated a pan-European empire. There are thinkers on the Alt Right today, like Richard Spencer, who advocate some form of this. You two have done a little bit of battle on that question, and you favor a more particularized ethnic nationalism, and he hopes for a more utopian universalism from Vladivostok to San Francisco.

What is your position on that question, ethnic nationalism as opposed to a sort of universal white empire, rooted in? Do you worry that the uniqueness of French culture and German culture and so forth will be subsumed under this larger formation? Or are you really just saying that people are not ready for this, and they will fight you over it, and they're not going to give that up? So forget about it.

Second, will the set of ideas collected around the Alt Right turn out to be a specifically American version of White Nationalism? It seems to me that white Americans and ethnic Europeans in Europe, nationalists in those places are facing different challenges.

The ethnic French nationalists are concerned with protecting and defending a French people and a French culture with deep historical roots and a cultural mythology that they want to protect from the corrosive effects of modernity or capitalism or immigration or what have you.

American White Nationalists seem to me to be engaged in a project of trying to awaken or build or rally a new national identity altogether. Because it's true that America was a white country for a long time. But as I was just talking about, that white population was never really unified.

The northern English basically made war on the Scots-Irish in the South for a long time. Some people would say that that continues today. Irish and Italians and Southern Europeans were all at various points considered outsiders. And now that's no longer the case. Everybody's sort of intermarried and interbred, and there really is a sort of a white culture in America today, even though the Irish and Italians have their little cultural things that they do.

Yet the vast majority of white Americans do not consider themselves a unique people apart from the civic nationalism of the United States. So are American White Nationalists engaged in a very different program from the European nationalists? And, and is the Alt Right maybe coming together to address those specific challenges?

GJ: Those are related questions, obviously. I wrote a short piece called "Why 'White' Nationalism?" I'm both an ethnonationalist and a White Nationalist. I'm an ethnonationalist in the sense that I think that we need to preserve distinct ethnic identities, distinct nations like France and Estonia. That's very important.[3]

But I don't exclude the United States from that. In the United States we have created an American identity. It's basically been created by mixing together people from various European stocks who weren't all that different to begin with. But a lot of them had to give up their ethnicity, their roots, and so forth to become Americans. They were deracinated and homogenized into something new. And that new thing isn't so terribly bad. I'm an American, and there's nothing else I can be.

There's a line in *Brideshead Revisited* where Julia says about her husband that she thought he was a whole man, but she realized that no, he's only a small part of a man grown monstrously large. Now he was a Canadian, but in that respect they're basically the same as Americans. Yes, there is something about Americans and Canadians and Australians and other basically European colonial societies that's a little monstrous.

Why is that? These societies were founded by people who were willing to sever their ties with their homelands. We were founded by rootless people. We were also founded by quarrelsome people, religious fanatics. And those traits are partly genetic. So rootlessness and quarrelsomeness are bred into the American character.

We're also, of course, very bourgeois. We don't have an aristocracy here. We were founded by people who were coming to the New World to better themselves materially or to escape to a place where they could practice their own particular religious denomination. I guess those are two small parts of the human being grown monstrously large: the tendency to be religious nonconformists and materialists. The materialism is really triumphant. But even the religious nonconformism was highly materialistic, Calvinism and so forth. The religion has faded into a culture of moralism and posturing. But the bourgeois element is

---

[3] Greg Johnson, "Why 'White' Nationalism?," in *Toward a New Nationalism* (San Francisco: Counter-Currents, 2019).

undimmed and enormously powerful. These are real problems.

And yet for all that, Americans have achieved great things. We certainly deserve to survive as a people. We deserve to have a future like the peoples of Europe. And I'm fighting for that future. I want Americans to have a future, and it's going to be in a white homeland in North America.

Now to this business about white imperialism versus ethnonationalism. I was very alarmed when Richard Spencer started talking about a "homogeneous European man." I'm sorry, but that basically means deracinating and blending out of existence all the different European peoples. And that's something like what happened in the European colonial societies.

That's what a white American is. A homogeneous European man. And indeed, Irish Americans and Italian Americans have St. Patrick's Day and Columbus Day. But let's be honest; let's be real here. A lot of this is LARPing. A guy says he's Irish American because he's got an Irish surname. But I know people who claim to be Irish Americans, and they're a quarter Irish and three quarters Italian. But they have an Irish surname. So they're "Irish" American. I know Italian Americans who have an Italian surname, but they're a quarter Italian and three quarters something else. So hyphenated-American ethnic identity is often just LARPing as something because you bear an ethnically identifiable surname, and that's it.

And if you look at the people who go to Saint Patrick's Day and to Octoberfest, they're the same people. Also an "Irish" American has more in common with a "Polish" American or an "Anglo" American than he has with somebody who lives in Ireland today. In terms of language, in terms of food, even in terms of general culture, they feel at home in the company of one another, and they feel like foreigners if they're in Ireland or Poland or England or whatever. That's just the reality of the situation.

So to say, like Vox Day has said to me several times, there is no such thing as a generic white American. They're Italian Americans and Irish Americans. I don't think that's true. There was a time when that was true, but that time has gone. That was then, this is now.

From the viewpoint of the European who is descended from

people who didn't up stakes and move to the New World because they wanted a better life, more stuff—from the viewpoint of a Frenchman or a Hungarian or anybody who's rooted and stayed behind—an American is a monster of rootlessness and homogenization. They're not going to allow that to happen in Europe. They don't want to become homogeneous European men. They want to be French or Hungarian or Latvian. And they have got every reason and right to do so. So they're going to veto this imperium idea.

DC: They will kill and die to prevent that.

GJ: They will kill and die to prevent it. So it's never going to happen. When Richard Spencer talks about "the ethnostate," he uses it in the singular, because he thinks of just one state. Well, the one ethnos for that single ethnostate has to be homogeneous European man. He doesn't think of the Czech Republic as an ethnostate. That's just Richard envisioning Russian tanks in the streets of Prague. He'll deny that. But he who wills the end has to will the means.

I tell everyone who says Europe should be united: Great, you put the Czechs and the Slovaks back together in the same state again, and then we'll talk. You put the Serbs and the Croats back together in the same state again, and then we'll talk. It's not going to happen. It's just grandiose and empty. Do we want Serbs and Croats to start fighting with one another again? Absolutely not. That's a horrible thing. Then don't force them to live under the same state.

The end of communism was horribly mismanaged by the Bush I administration. They said "We stand for stability," the stability of multinational, multi-ethnic empires against nations yearning to be free of communist tyranny. What horrible fools Bush I and his people were. When the communist regime fell in Yugoslavia, or when it was falling apart in Russia, the United States should have stood for the liberty of all the different peoples in that vast prison house of nations that was the Soviet bloc. We should have stood up for the peaceful partition and secession of distinct ethnostates.

But instead of doing that, we suffered a decade of wars in the

Balkans, so that they could end up with such states. We should have just gone straight there in a diplomatic way. That would have been the best thing.

So if you don't want Serbs and Croats to fight again, don't force them to have the same state over them. Do we want to prevent wars between European peoples? Then don't force them to have the same government over them.

Now what if they want to fight anyway? That's when you need a Pan-European sensibility. Because we are all Europeans. That's a racial sensibility, a sense of our common whiteness. So even in a Europe of proud little ethnostates, there's room for a sense of overarching whiteness and Europeaness, and that's real. So if tensions start rising between the Hungarians and the Romanians somewhere down the road, the other states in Europe need to step in and say, "We need to walk this back."

There's a concept from the ancient world. It's called "the King's Peace." After two attempts to conquer mainland Greece, by Darius and Xerxes, the Persians gave up on that. Yet Artaxerxes II found a way of extending Persian influence into mainland Greece without actually ruling over it. He extended hegemony, soft power, by basically saying that if any Greek city-state attacked another, he would put the full weight of the Persian Empire on the side of the attacked party. It was not a perfect solution, but it did reduce fighting between the notoriously quarrelsome mainland Greek city-states for two decades. That was a great gift.

The ideology of the Persian Empire is that it created peace between warring peoples that could not create peace between themselves because they were too well-matched in battle, so one could never conquer the other. But they could be pacified by an overwhelming third force. The Persians fought for glory and wealth, of course. But Cyrus also legitimated his conquests by pacifying peoples weary of war but unable to conclude peace on their own by forcing them to get along. That's why Cyrus was the first "prince of peace," a title later transferred to Jesus.

Peace was the ideology of the Persian empire. But you don't actually need to rule others to resolve conflicts. You just need a pan-European sensibility. The most nationalistic people I know in every European society realize there's something terribly tragic about Europeans killing one another. Because as a race we have so much more in common. Every European society is threatened with negative population growth. Every European society is threatened with invasion from non-Europeans. That's far more important than little border disputes that can be solved without bloodshed.

The closest thing to a European imperium that would be both desirable and practical is a non-sovereign intergovernmental treaty organization, something like NATO, in which European nations ally together out of two common interests: to maintain peace among themselves and to maintain advantageous relations with other racial and civilizational blocs, like the Muslim world, Africa, Far East, etc. There needs to be some kind of co-ordination. So something like NATO, without the United States or Russia in it, an actual European NATO, would be the best solution. But it would be totally consistent with maintaining the distinct sovereign ethnostates that exist in Europe today.

DC: I would say for a lot of Americans on the Right, the biggest and last stumbling block is the Jewish question. What is the Jewish question? Why does it merit being named clearly and separately as opposed to just sort of being an obvious fact following from ethnonationalism in general?

GJ: Well I actually wrote a piece called "Reframing the Jewish Question," where I say that it is just a first-order implication of ethnonationalism.[4]

DC: That's poor preparation right there.

GJ: What you said reflects a very common attitude amongst White Nationalists. They always say first we start with ethnonationalism and realism about race. But the Jewish thing is like higher mathematics. It's like advanced calculus. We don't have to go there right away. My response is no, it's not advanced calculus. It's a first-order self-evident implication of the ethnona-

---

[4] Greg Johnson, "Reframing the Jewish Question," *Toward a New Nationalism*.

tionalist principle, which is that the best way to prevent conflicts between different peoples to the extent that that's possible is for them to have their sovereign homelands.

And lo and behold, Jews actually struggled for a very long time to create a sovereign Jewish homeland, namely Israel. And my attitude is that Jews should live in their sovereign homeland. But they don't, because they're not forced to. And because it's very advantageous for them to have it both ways. They have their ethnostate, and they also live as a diaspora. Now the ethnostate benefits from that, because the diaspora is constantly meddling in the internal affairs of their host societies to support Israel.

That's especially true in the United States, where we have as many Jews living as in Israel, and Israel gets billions of dollars every year in loans and just outright giveaways and loans that will never be paid back. So they're just giveaways. Americans have also wasted our people's blood and trillions of dollars since 2003 fighting wars in the Middle East that are dictated by Israeli strategic calculations. I won't even dignify it by saying that it's in their interest. But certainly they calculated it to be in their interests. US interests simply didn't enter in. It is absolutely catastrophic that our foreign policy is controlled by people who are thinking primarily about the interests of a foreign society, namely Israel, rather than the good of America.

Jews are a distinct people, and they're loyal to one another, and that's all healthy and well and good. But if that's true, then we cannot give them citizenship in our societies, power in our societies, and influence over our societies at the same time. That is what the Jewish question is. That Jewish question arose with the emancipation of Jewish communities in Europe. For a very long time they were encapsulated self-governing communities. Then they were "emancipated" by Napoleon. He was the great emancipator of Jewry.

As soon as Jews were emancipated and became citizens of the societies around them, people raised a question: "Not only are Jews citizens of our society, with all the rights of citizens, they're also, in fact, citizens of their own society. Their primary loyalty is to other Jews all around the world, in even in our rival societies, even in enemy societies, even in societies we're fighting wars against. Isn't there something weird about this? Isn't this an inherently unjust and disadvantageous relationship that we've instituted?"

Let's look at this in terms of game theory. Just as a team strategy beats an individualistic strategy, if you've got somebody with dual citizenship, basically, that dual citizenship is a way that their team can play you. They can hack your system. And as the nineteenth and twentieth centuries unfolded, we saw that pattern over and over again. Influential Jewish minorities in various European societies caused wars and revolutions and catastrophic policies for the societies that they were ostensibly citizens of and thus ostensibly should have been looking out for their common good.

But naturally Jews are more concerned with their real nation, the Jewish nation. Thus when the interests of their two nations conflict, they tend to side with the Jewish nation. Which is a very bad for their host societies, because Jews tend to be upwardly mobile and highly influential. Therefore, they tend to be well-placed to subvert the interests of their host societies.

In the nineteenth century, influential Jews in Germany were playing really dangerous games, shifting German foreign policy in Eastern Europe to be advantageous to Eastern European Jewry. Today, influential Jews shift American foreign policy to be beneficial to Israel. That shouldn't be possible. We shouldn't allow foreign peoples to influence our institutions for the benefit of foreign powers.

It doesn't matter if they're Right-wing Jews or Left-wing Jews. The pattern is the same. There's a story in the Old Testament, in the book of Genesis. It is the story of Jacob and Esau. One Jew has wronged another. Jacob has wronged Esau, his half-brother. Years later, Jacob sees Esau's clan approaching his clan. He doesn't know if Esau means ill or not. He fears being attacked. So to ensure his survival, he divides his camp. He sends some of his people to the other camp as defectors. The role of these defectors is to influence the enemy camp. And if the enemy camp attacks the home camp and destroys it, at least some of the home camp will survive among the enemy.

If you look at the history of Jewish intellectual movements and Jewish political involvement since Jewish emancipation, you see this pattern over and over. The neoconservatives are a beautiful example of this. The main population of neoconservatives comes out of the Zionist wing of the Trotskyite movement. Bolshevism was largely a Jewish thing. Marx was a Jew. The core people who advanced Bolshevism were Jews or part-Jews or married to Jews. It was a heavily Jewish phenomenon. The most ethnically conscious Jews ended up following Trotsky, and the most ethnically conscious Trotskyites became Zionists, and Zionist Trotskyites at a certain point "defected," from the Left to the Right and became conservatives during the Cold War.

As the neocons colonized the Republican Party, like cuckoos, they ejected the eggs and the hatchlings of real conservatives from the nest. They mopped it up pretty thoroughly. They destroyed the careers of a lot of actual conservatives, non-Jewish, non-neocons. Who were some of these hatchlings, these bonafide conservatives who are ejected from the nest along the way? The whole John Birch Society was read out in the 1960s. Then people like Joseph Sobran and Peter Brimelow were ejected.

Once the neocons took over the Right in America, they turned it into a vehicle for advancing Jewish interests around the world, especially in the Middle East. The neocons are pushing and have pushed these catastrophic wars in the Middle East. Now that Trump has come along, they don't feel comfortable, in the Republican Party. So they're just reinventing themselves as Democrats, because the foreign policy of Hillary Clinton's party has always been controlled by the same faction.

How do you make sure that American foreign policy is always pro-Jewish? You divide your camp and you colonize both the Republicans and the Democrats, so that no matter who's in power, they have a pro-Zionist foreign policy. When Democrats are in power, they go through the charade of the "peace process," because Democratic voters want peace. You know, the peace process that never eventuates in peace and always requires more American money to keep the whole thing going. When Republicans are in power, it's a more truculent approach, where we're actually fighting wars, because Republicans sublimate all their warlike and fascist impulses into Zionism. But it's the same group of people running American foreign policy, exercising veto power over American foreign policy for the ethnic interests of Israel.

Enough is enough. We cannot trust these people to actually look out for the interests of America. So they need to go. They need to go to their homeland and become a normal people. We need to rigorously police their agents and friends in America so that they're not subverting American foreign policy away from American interests and towards Israeli interests. It's really as simple as that. I wish Jews all the best, but I cannot like them, and I cannot regard them in a friendly way until they relinquish power over our society and stop egging it on towards catastrophic foreign policy disasters.

Jews also play a huge role in promoting every form of Left-liberal decadence and decline that sensible conservatives have to oppose: race-mixing, gay lib, women's lib, multiculturalism, porn, drugs, and so forth. They're shorting Western civilization, meaning they're profiting from the decline of our values. They've set themselves up in our society to profit from our decline. They profit from the decline of our families. They profit from the decline of our sexual behavior and morality. They profit from the decline of our institutions. Our marriages are breaking up? Well, you know, that's great for lawyers.

So overall I think that Jews play an incredibly negative role in American society and other European societies. But there's no reason, though, why we should have these conflicts with them, because they have a homeland of their own. They need to go there and live there and flourish there.

DC: I don't quite understand the multiculturalism aspect of it, especially not in the United States where we have a different type of Muslim population, a large enough country where it's not quite a problem. But from what I understand, Jewish groups and Jewish voters in European countries are pretty much fully on board with importing as many refugees as they can. I don't understand what they would get out of that, because I can't imagine anybody that's going to be more tolerant of them as a group than especially an Anglo-Protestant society, but European in general. Do you have any thoughts on that?

GJ: Jews have long memories. They constantly try to goose our memory with Holocaust education, because it's their contention that a European society within living memory tried to exterminate every last one of them and conquer the world. Now there's a lot of malarkey connected with that claim, but a lot of Jews fervently believe that. They believe that Europeans are capable of trying to exterminate every last one of them. Whereas Jews have lived in very cordial relations with Muslims for very long periods of time. They chose to put their ethnostate in a sea of Muslims, which is very interesting. They could have gone to Uganda or Madagascar or the Soviet Far East. But they chose to live in a sea of Muslims. They're not as afraid of Muslims as they are of us. And that's basically the reason. Therefore, they feel greater fear in homogeneous European societies than they do in a sea of Muslims in Israel. That's fascinating. That might not be rational, but that's how they feel.

Jews promote multiculturalism because they are an outsider group. Hence they don't want you to think of yourself as belonging to a Christian society because they're not Christians. They don't want to live in an ethnically defined society, because there are different ethnic group. Thus they have worked tirelessly to open up the borders not only of the United States, but of every European society to nonwhite immigration. Why? Because as the European majority is diluted, their power grows. It's as simple as that.

Now, a lot of people say, "But these Muslims beat up Jewish schoolboys. They're dangerous people." Yes, that's true. But every day Israel makes and enforces policies that they know will cause terrorism directed at Jews. Every day they do that. They know that a certain number of Jews are going to die because of the policies they enact. But they're willing to accept that. They're willing to accept that within the borders of their own state. So they're certainly willing to accept it in France. They're certainly willing to accept it in the United States. Because they think it redounds on balance to the greater good of their community, and they're willing to accept a few casualties. It's as simple as that.

DC: Just like in any country, when a president needs support, he starts a war, when Jewish emancipation happened in Europe, a lot of the conservative rabbis and people who were really committed to the community were more afraid of assimilation than they were of extermination or violence. Creating a certain level of conflict firms up the boundaries and the membranes between peoples.

GJ: This is true, this is very true. And assimilation is a great threat to Jews. All traits are distributed along bell curves, and that includes genetic traits like ethnocentrism. Like other people who are predominantly Middle Eastern, Jews as an ethnic group are more ethnocentric than Europeans. This is just a fact of reality. It's biologically clear. But those traits are distributed on bell curves, and the less ethnocentric Jews will marry out.

I've known a number of them. I've had Jewish friends. Over the years, I've allowed them to drop, and some of them died. I've not tried to make new Jewish friendships, because as I became increasingly aware of the Jewish problem, I just didn't want to have these sticky dual loyalties in my own life.

One of these friends actually gave me "permission" to think a lot of these thoughts. In fact, she egged me on. She had a very interesting life. She was an orphan. She had every reason to believe her parents were killed in the Holocaust. She was raised as Catholic, and she only discovered that she was Jewish when she was a teenager. This Jewish family showed up and said that she was part of the family. They took her away from the Catholic orphanage where she was being raised. She wanted to be a nun when she grew up. They told her she was a Jew and tried to make her into a Jew.

She told me that being turned into a Jew basically meant being turned into a misanthrope who hated the rest of humanity, stayed indoors all the time, and didn't go out and play. When she wasn't inclined to do that, they actually started calling her "the little German." And after a while, *they took her back to the orphanage and dumped her*. That's a really fascinating story. But she was one of these low-ethnocentrism Jews. She ended up marrying out. She married a white guy. She had kids, and she didn't even tell her children about her Jewish heritage until they were all grown up.

That's an example of the kind of people who marry out. You can only really have barriers to that if there's a great deal of polarization in society between Jews and gentiles. So yes, the Jewish community needs antisemitism to affirm its boundaries. That's why they're constantly searching for it with a magnifying glass and tweezers.

I love Yoav Shamir's documentary *Defamation*, where he went to the offices of the Anti-Defamation League in New York, where they collect antisemitic horror stories, maybe sixty or eighty a day. Fortunately, the vast majority are quite trivial. People calling in complaining they weren't allowed to take Jewish holidays off. It's antisemitism! These people don't feel privileged enough. They're objectively the most privileged group in America, but not privileged enough by their own lights. So they have an organization that has hundreds of millions of dollars a year, where they can snitch on their employers for not giving them even more special treatment than they already get.

This is antisemitism, but they need this. They need this consciousness to maintain their boundaries. Yet a lot of Jews are choosing to marry out and cease to be Jewish. You can't blame them. A lot of them just want to join the human race, rather than be misanthropes, which is what their religion requires. So Jews need antisemitism to survive as a separate group.

Yet at the same time, they have this weird reflexive habit of constantly racking their brains to figure out where antisemitism comes from. I remember Natan Sharansky wrote a book that of all people, George W. Bush praised. It may have been the second book he ever read after the children's book on 9/11. I read some excerpts of it on the web, and I was howling with laughter because he says antisemitism is the most baffling thing. There's no common denominator. It happens in Buddhist societies and Christian societies. It happens in Muslim societies. It's happened in every stage of history. Under capitalism, socialism, and Communism. There's no common denominator. But wait a second, there's one thing that all of these societies have in common, and that's Jews. Israel Shahak said the ghettos grew up because they existed in the minds of Jews. They were just an externalization of the Jewish mentality, of their own separateness and their insistence on being separate. Their dietary laws, their dual ethical codes, all these things are designed to maintain their sense of separateness and distinctness as a people. But that separateness and the tendency to look down upon other people as not really human does inevitably produce a backlash. And we call that antisemitism. Jews are aware of their own Jewishness. When gentiles become aware of Jewishness, it often takes the form of antisemitism.

DC: In 1903 or 1904, Theodor Herzl, the father of modern political Zionism, was at a British governmental panel on immigration giving testimony. One of the people asked him what his definition of a nation was. I can't remember the exact quote, but he said something to the effect that it's a recognizable group of common cohesion, united by a common enemy. And he asked him, so what's the common enemy? And he said, to the Jew, it's the anti-Semite. When I read that, I thought to myself, if your sense of social identity is completely tied to the presence of this enemy, this implacable universal enemy, the question that obviously pops up is what happens to you if there's no antisemitism left? And the answer is that can't ever happen.

GJ: They can't allow that to happen. So they conjure up the anti-Semite. It's a necessary prop of their existence. If they can't conjure up real ones, they conjure up fake ones. Which is why so many anti-Jewish acts of vandalism turn out to be fake hate crimes created by Jews. In fact, they are real hate crimes committed against gentiles.

DC: What about people like the woman you knew? I guess that's a question a lot of people have. In fact, a friend of mine here in Orange County is half-Japanese and half-Jewish, but outside of that fact, he would fit perfectly on the Alt Right. He sounds like you without the White Nationalist part. In the society that you envision . . . I guess you sort of answered this question earlier. You don't want to throw that guy out. You want to control immigration and then just slowly over the course of a generation or two have the demographics change, right?

GJ: You have your amiable Asian friends. A lot of White Nationalists have amiable Asian friends. You don't want to be mean to these people, but at the same time, we don't want to continue down a road where our people have no future. There's no danger of Asians becoming extinct. They exist in vast numbers. They have their own sovereign homelands. Yet at the same time, there's a grave danger that whites will go extinct. I know it sounds catastrophic and alarmist, but it's actually very simple math. Every year, more of us die than are being born, and if that doesn't change, there will be none of us eventually.

One of the ways that we don't reproduce ourselves is by miscegenation. A lot of us reproduce, but we don't reproduce our race because we marry out. People who are conservative find Asians very tempting because of their brightness, their orderliness, and their capacity to create high civilizations and appreciate our own.

We need to have barriers to that. Over a few generations if we erect those kinds of barriers, it will cease to be an issue. That's really all I have to say about that. I'm not one of these people who faps and drools to race war propaganda scenarios and that kind of nonsense. I just think that's unnecessary, and it's gross. Our aim is to prevent racial conflict, not encourage it.

DC: It's usually fake. I've met some of those people. If I put them in a room with a gun and a black person and said, "Do your thing," they would not do it. It's LARPing a lot of the time. They like the thrill of verbal taboo-breaking, shocking people, being that guy. I don't really have a lot of patience with them. That's why I'm talking to you as opposed to maybe somebody else.

GJ: I wrote this piece called "Tough Talk from a Hard Man (On the Internet)."[5] A lot of these people are just tough talkers,

---

[5] Greg Johnson, "Tough Talk from a Hard Man (on the Internet)," *Toward a New Nationalism*.

posturing as hard men on the internet. I'm sorry, but we have to take it off the Internet. We have to be real. We have to think about solutions that are sensible and moral and decent and fair. There's nothing fairer than allowing every people to have a land of its own.

DC: If the Alt Right continues to grow in power on the American Right, we're probably going to have to ditch the word "conservative" and bring back "reactionary," because the way you phrase it, it's a defensive response to something that you see happening, and a line needs to be drawn.

GJ: Yeah.

DC: It's not an attack. It's a defensive position in a way.

GJ: Yeah. But I don't like the idea of being called a reactionary or being a reactionary. Yes, it's a reaction. It's self-defense. But reactionary has a connotation of cranks who don't want to use computers. They want to use quill pens. People who not only LARP, but LARP as seventeenth-century puritans.

DC: I've seen some of them going on about America needing to be a Catholic country. I'm like, what are you talking about? Are we on the same planet? It might happen if we continue our immigration from the south. That's making us more Catholic. But that's the only way it's happening.

GJ: Yeah, exactly. I get a good chuckle out of that kind of stuff. Actually, I don't think of myself as a reactionary at all. I think my policies, to be honest, are closer to the Progressive Movement of the earlier twentieth century than to anything that's reactionary. They believed in eugenics. They believed in nature preservation. They passed immigration restriction. A lot of them were influenced by Darwinism. That's all good.

A lot of these people recognized that the things that made America great, which are not captured by thin concepts like liberalism and democracy. The things that made America great at the end of the nineteenth and the beginning of the twentieth century were ethnically specific. They were connected with the ethnic genetic interests of northern Europeans, and they wanted to preserve that. That's me, up one side and down the other. That's how I feel about politics. They also believed in regulating capitalism to serve the common good. I believe that too. So in some ways I'm a throwback to the Progressive Movement.

I like Guillaume Faye's book *Archeofuturism* because he is progressive in some ways—he believes in technology and progress in those senses—but he realizes that these things need to be infused by a return of archaic values, meaning pre-liberal, pre-modern values. What that means aside from, say, healthy attitudes about the differences between the sexes, are classical aristocratic values, pre-bourgeois values. I think that's absolutely right.

I wrote a piece about Frank Herbert's *Dune* as a kind of archeofuturist science fiction novel. Herbert was thinking about what form of society is consistent with mankind rising to the stars and colonizing the galaxy, and he concluded very rapidly it wasn't going to be liberal democracy. It had to be an aristocratic society with immensely long time horizons, so he modeled it on medieval European society, where holy orders and dynasties and aristocratic families thought far into the future. They had enormous time horizons, as opposed to today, when corporations think about the next quarter and politicians think about the next election, and all serious problems are just kicked down the road to somebody else. That's no way to go to the stars.

DC: I think a lot of the people who are new arrivals to the Alt Right, and even just Trump voters, are former conservatives and or libertarians. I was a libertarian, and you get to the point where you realize that it wasn't the Civil War or 1776 or any of those that were really our finest hour. I think I've heard you say that the American labor movement in a lot of ways was our finest hour. And as a libertarian, you vomit when you hear that, but . . .

GJ: I know. But there's so much truth to that. My view about labor unions is basically this: In a badly ordered society, where you don't have a wise leadership that's looking out for the common good, labor unions are the best way of moving accidentally, through negotiation and clashes between different interest groups, toward a good society. First of all, we need constant pressure towards technological progress, and that means keeping labor costs high. That's the way that we avoid the plantation economy, which is the evilest form of Anglo-Saxon capitalism. And that's what globalization is producing today. A global plantation economy. We need the pressure towards technological progress.

DC: I was very happy to hear Peter Thiel allude to that.

GJ: Yes, he sees that, very clearly. The other thing that the labor movement does is make sure that the productivity gains of technological progress go to the working and middle classes. We do not want the wealth generated by all these technological productivity gains to be just hoarded by some vastly wealthy people, because that creates a dangerously unrepublican form of government.

As I outlined in an essay called "Money for Nothing,"[6] the ultimate goal of forcing technological progress, and forcing the productivity gains of technological progress to go back to the workers, would be a society where machines put us all out of work. Because if we had a society where machines put us all out of work in the present dispensation, everyone would starve, and then the capitalists would starve too.

DC: And then they would get their heads cut off.

GJ: Yeah. Perhaps they think that when the workers die off, they can create machines that will pay them to consume the products of other machines. It's a totally ludicrous vision of things, but it is what we get when we lose track of the fact that the only purpose of the economy is to enable humans to live well.

How do we get to the *Star Trek* economy or *The Jetsons* economy? An economy where productivity gains are cashed out, not in terms of increased consumption, because we live on a finite planet. So it has to be cashed out in terms of increased leisure. Until we're working one hour a week, or something like that,

---

[6] Greg Johnson, "Money for Nothing," *Truth, Justice, & a Nice White Country* (San Francisco: Counter-Currents, 2015).

and all living at comfortable Western middle-class standards.

What do you do with the rest of your time? Explore the cosmos, improve recipes, plant gardens, raise kids, strum guitars, whatever. That's what I would like to see happen. And I think that the clash between labor and capital was pushing things in that direction in America before globalization, when we opened up the borders to in-sourcing the Third World and shipping factories to the Third World. That's pushing us in the direction of a global plantation economy. It has taken the mainspring out of the forces driving us towards constant technological improvement. Except technological improvement in computing. Computers make us more productive, but they are also ways that we amuse ourselves in a declining society. Let's just be honest about that.

We need to stop the slide toward the global plantation economy. We need to return to a high-wage, high-tech economy that produces a broad middle class and evolves eventually into a society where everybody's basically out of work, because machines produce everything at virtually no expense. But instead of being starving unemployed workers, we will all be collecting dividends, basically because everyone will be part of the capitalist class. This is how we get to the post-scarcity utopia that utopian socialists were babbling about in the nineteenth century. That can actually happen.

I'd like to see that kind of *Star Trek* world. The economic theory that can lead us there is called Social Credit. I explain it in the essay "Money for Nothing," which is in my book, *Truth, Justice, and a Nice White Country*. I'm sure there are friends of yours who are gasping at that title. I hope so.

Social Credit, before it was cast down the memory hole, was the preferred economic theory of Anglophone fascists from Canada and the United States and England all the way to Australia and New Zealand. It was a huge thing before it disappeared after World War II. There's a whole undiscovered continent of Right-wing critics of unregulated capitalism out there.

Counter-Currents, July 25–August 2, 2019

WHITE IDENTITY POLITICS

INTERVIEW WITH
TARA MCCARTHY*

TARA MCCARTHY: Welcome back to *Reality Calls*. Today I'm talking with Greg Johnson, who is the editor of *Counter-Currents*.

GREG JOHNSON: Thank you for having me on.

TM: Yes, thanks for joining me. We're going to talk about White Nationalism, because you identify as a White Nationalist. I thought it'd be interesting to talk about what that is and why you identify that way. Would you mind starting by telling us what your view of White Nationalism is?

GJ: Certainly. White Nationalism is just the idea that the best political order is a patchwork of sovereign nation-states for ethnically distinct peoples. The larger principle, which we call ethnonationalism, of course applies to any race. Being white myself, and being concerned about demographic and political trends that are threatening the future of white people worldwide, I'm most concerned about whites. I think that White Nationalism—meaning ethnostates for different white peoples—is really the best solution to staving-off the long-term demographic problems that whites are facing.

There's a widespread misconception that White Nationalism means the idea that all white people belong in the same state. I think that that's a ridiculous idea, a parody actually, of what most White Nationalists believe. Most White Nationalists believe that the nation-state is the natural political unit—the most functional political unit, the one that's most consistent with

---

* Transcript of an interview for the *Reality Calls* YouTube channel recorded in mid-March of 2017.

maintaining peace among different peoples and also conditions where different peoples can develop and live according to their own view of what's right. We are all for preserving differences and borders between white peoples.

The great conflicts of the twentieth century were largely between different white nations. Largely those conflicts came about because some groups did not respect the autonomy of other white groups. First and foremost, we would like to have peace between our own peoples. Then after that, we need to also deal with the threats posed by large geopolitical and racial blocs of rivals to European peoples.

The biggest threat to Europe, of course, is the Islamic world. Europe is being invaded by Muslims. These Muslims are there with the very conscious design of spreading their religion and political order to Europe. They're quite open and frank about that. It really does constitute a somewhat slow and stealthy invasion.

But many invasions in the past have been slow and stealthy conquests by demographic replacement. They're not necessarily armies blitzing over borders. When you look at the end of the Roman Empire, that came about because the Romans thought it was a really clever idea to bring in Germanic tribes and settle them in Roman lands. They enlisted them in their legions. They'll do jobs that Romans won't do.

When Rome was sacked, it wasn't sacked by people who came from outside the empire but primarily by barbarians who were living within its borders. They'd finally had enough of being ruled by a very effete and corrupt elite that they held in contempt. So the process of invasion by demographic replacement that's going on today is not something all that unusual in history.

In the United States, the main problem is invasion from the global south, especially Latin America. The Canadians are also happily importing people from everywhere. But for the US the primary problem is the invasion of Latin Americans, largely nonwhite mestizos or Indians.

What we need is white distinction and diversity where we have our own little homelands, and we need a certain amount of coordination and unity and solidarity when facing geopolitical threats from nonwhite groups. There's also, of course, the Chinese question and South Asia, Africa, and so forth. These are distinct groups of people, distinct geopolitical blocs, and it would be nice if white nations coordinated their plans regarding them in order to survive, rather than what we have today, which is our leadership conspiring to replace our population with nonwhites from around the world.

TM: So one objection I suppose people might have to this idea of, "We're being replaced" is "Well, we're all the same anyway, so what does it matter?" What is your perspective on that?

GJ: Well, wait a second, I thought that diversity was a wonderful thing? [laughter] The same people who say we're all the same and it doesn't matter are also the ones who say, "Oh, isn't it wonderful that we can get shawarma in London now?" "Isn't it wonderful that we have pygmy restaurants?" I don't know if you actually have pygmy restaurants yet. But wouldn't it be wonderful if abos, pygmies, and other groups like that opened up little restaurants in West London somewhere? Wouldn't that be chic and interesting?

The Left—and it's not really just the Left, it's the globalist establishment—are promoting multiculturalism and nonwhite immigration. They really speak with forked tongues. Nonwhite immigrants are simultaneously people who have low skills and people with great skills who will do the important professional jobs that white people just won't do. They're also peaceful and law-abiding people, far less criminal than native Europeans. They say that diversity is a wonderful thing that only makes us stronger. Then they say we are all the same, and our differences don't matter anyway.

At a certain point you just have to conclude that these people are not honest. But if they're not honest, you've got to stop listening to them. Eventually you've got to simply defeat them politically to prevent them from doing what they're doing.

That's one of the hardest things for white people to wrap

their minds around: that people in positions of power might be simply self-interested, Machiavellian liars.

Granted, there's a lot of shallow, facile cynicism about politics. But oddly enough, people still seem to have a great difficulty wrapping their minds around what you would actually do if you really believed that our leaders are lying to us, that they have very evil ulterior motives that they're pushing.

When you look at the contradictions of the globalist rhetoric—the Left is for globalism because of socialism, and the Right is for globalism because of capitalism—but they all promote the same ultimate end, which is a giant plantation economy ruled over by a fabulously wealthy and corrupt elite, you have to start wondering about the sincerity of the voices putting forward the same conclusions with a whole raft of different arguments directed at different constituencies.

The common denominator, though, is that they're trying to swindle the native peoples of all European lands—and also European colonial peoples like Americans, Canadians, etc.—of having a future, of having homelands where they can be confident that they will control the government, control their destiny, and feel like they are at home, as opposed to something that is increasingly like a Middle Eastern bazaar in parts of London, or increasingly like Latin America in large parts of the United States.

TM: I've got a few questions here. I've asked my audience to ask you. When I asked them to submit questions, some of them were quite rude and automatically wanted to make a point about how much they objected to even asking you questions [laughter]. But most of them were quite willing to ask questions. So I'm going to give a few a shot, and I've actually got a lot of them, so if you could give a fairly brief response.

What life experiences formed your worldview? What was your home life like growing up and through school?

GJ: I grew up in a very homogenously white community, and it was only when I went off to college that I was exposed to different groups of people, and my initial assumption was that we're all basically the same, and we can all live together the same way I lived growing up in a small homogeneously white town.

I discovered very quickly that that's not the attitude of many minorities in the United States. Many of them have a great deal of distrust and hostility toward whites and look at us as people to victimize. There's also a lot of subtle mockery and passive aggression in day-to-day interactions.

So eventually I started realizing that this is not actually working. I realized that my "multicultural phase," if you will, was rooted in projecting my own mentality on the rest of the world. There's a deep form of hubris and ethnocentrism that is present in multiculturalism.

The first form of multiculturalism is the "white man's burden" idea. It's the imperialist idea that all of these people really want to be like us. So we're going to go out and give them the benefits of our civilization, because all good things come from white people. We're going to share those gifts with them, whether they want it or not.

The flip-side of that is the guilty, Leftist, anti-colonialist white mentality, which is just as grandiose, because instead of assuming that all good things come from whites — and nonwhites don't have any agency of their own and have nothing of their own that they'd want to hold on to — this Leftist mentality blames us for all the bad things that happen to nonwhites. It's our fault. But this is based on the same grandiose notion that whites are the only people who matter in the world, for good or evil. Other people are negligible as agents. That is a deep, bedrock assumption of a lot of Leftists.

I stopped the projection and decided to try to understand the world as these people see it. I came to realize that a lot of peoples, in fact the majority of peoples on Earth, do not have a transparent and trusting relationship to other groups. In fact, they have suspicious, hostile, and manipulative relationships to other groups. But in white countries we're inviting in people on the assumption that they're going to be just like us, that we're going to be generous to them and open to them, and they're going to be open and generous to us.

In fact, they think we are incredibly weak and naïve. They will dissimulate belief in our ideas when they want something from us. When we want something from them, they'll pretend to be fair. But they'll end up practicing ruthless ethnic nepotism. They've hacked us. They've hacked our minds. They're using our openness and goodness to exploit us. That puts us in a very disadvantageous position.

Imagine you're playing poker, and you have the biggest stack of chips, but everybody else at the table has a wild card, mainly the race card. But you don't think of yourself as a member of a race. You think of yourself as an avatar of universal humanity.

If you play that game, they're going to pull out the race card and use it in hand after hand after hand. They're going to have a systematic advantage in every hand that you play. You might have a very big stack of chips at the beginning, but you will lose everything if you keep playing by those stacked rules. That's how multiculturalism works. They have the race card. They can always play it. But we can't.

The beginning of white identity politics is getting whites to recognize that in multicultural societies the game is systematically rigged against them. We will lose if we play this game, if we don't take our own side, if we don't start playing the race card and thinking about our own collective interests as a group.

Once we start down that path, though, my hope is eventually we're going to see that it was quite wise and wonderful when Britain was virtually 100% white. And it was quite wise and wonderful when France was virtually 100% white. You didn't have alien groups swindling you out of your future.

And it's not just tiny, marginal groups like the stereotypical gypsies of the past who are doing this. It's now the upcoming majority, the rising majority in France and England. There are countries in Europe where there are more babies named Muhammed than any other name.

TM: Yup, that's the case in Ireland right now.

GJ: Yes, and that means in the long run you're going to be outbred in your own homelands in Europe — and in the United States and Canada as well — by people who are hostile and there to take away what we have created: to take away our wealth, to take away our civilization, to take away our future.

When I started realizing that was the game, and the long-term consequences were quite dire, I decided I can't be liberal anymore. I can't be an individualist anymore. Liberal individualism blinds us to the priority of ethnic politics, and if we don't break out of that mindset, we're going to lose everything that we've got.

Sorry that wasn't too brief. But I'll try to be briefer.

TM: That's okay. Actually, my follow up question is: Why do you think that you got this perspective? Because so many people have experienced very similar things to you, yet they haven't come around to your perspective, so why do you think that might be?

GJ: Because people are programmed not to see the problems. Beyond that, those who do see the problems are intimidated into not speaking about them. Moreover, people who see the problems often think nothing can be done. Or they are simply too selfish to do anything about them.

We are ruled by people who are promoting multiculturalism through every authoritative channel that molds opinions in society today. They're pushing this idea that white people are guilty for all the world's ills, and that if we're having difficulties with immigrant groups, that's somehow our fault, that we better keep quiet about it, that the worst possible sin is to be racist or ethnocentric. A lot of people are simply intimidated by this. They're intimidated into silence.

One thing that helps them maintain their silence, though, is the naïve assumption that somehow — if they make a separate peace with the system — things will work out fine for them. This is a "devil take the hindmost" form of individualism.

Most people are also short-term thinkers. They are unwilling to confront the fact that multiculturalism is rigged against us, that the long-term trends are quite dire, and that we simply will cease to exist as distinct nations and as a biological race in a couple hundred years if we don't stop this

So we're brainwashed, we're guilty, we're individualistic, we're afraid of joining together and actually trying to change things, we feel helpless and hopeless, and a lot of us are just ignorant of the long-term consequences of staying on this path. I think all of those things combined together prevent people who see the same things we do from actually drawing the right conclusions that we've got to do something about it.

I do, however, think all people are hard-wired for a certain level of ethnocentrism. That's been proven scientifically. It turns out that whites are the least ethnocentric race. And that means we are the most trusting and welcoming of outsiders. However, at a certain point we're going to stop feeling trusting and welcoming of outsiders because our ethnocentrism will kick in.

TM: I'm a little bit skeptical of that, having grown up in London. Whites are now less than 50% of the population in London, but I don't see that happening [laughter].

GJ: But would you agree that there are more people becoming ethnocentric today than there were?

TM: No. People in London, whites in London, were pro-remain in the EU, which puts us at risk of flooding the country with migrants because most of them want to come. They get residence in an EU country, and then once they've got that visa they move to the UK, and that's what they want to do, obviously because it's an English-speaking country.

Most of them speak English already to some extent—if they speak a second language, it's going to be English; it's not going to be Norwegian—that's why they prefer to come to the UK, and we're at risk of being flooded.

GJ: Well, how about this, what about the whites who have been leaving London over the past thirty years? Why are they leaving? They're probably going to give you euphemisms and stories like, "We wanted a quieter neighborhood," "We wanted better schools for our children," or whatever, which is the same kind of thing that you hear from whites who are fleeing diversity in the United States. But they're really fleeing diversity. That's how a lot of whites deal with this problem. They try to run away from it.

How many Britons live in Spain now?

TM: Lots. Yeah.

GJ: Hundreds of thousands, I think. That's an astonishing thing. I'd love to do a poll of those Britons who live in Spain. Why'd they move to Spain? Isn't it odd?

TM: The weather?

GJ: Yeah [laughter], "the weather," that's what they'd say. But isn't it odd that they seem to feel more at home amongst Spaniards than they do among people in their own country? But then you look at the people in their own country, the people who moved into their neighborhoods. They might not have been British. So there's a lot of white flight that goes on. Again, this is one way people avoid dealing with the problem. They just run away from it.

Germans are now moving to Hungary. Germany is importing Muslims. Germans who don't like that are fleeing to Hungary, which isn't importing Muslims. But that's really not good for Germany, and it's not good for Hungary either. The Hungarians are welcoming them because they're bringing money, but they should look at them as rats fleeing a sinking ship, rats fleeing a plague ship. Because a lot of the ideas that messed up Germany are probably lodged in the heads of Germans who are coming to Hungary. Pretty soon they'll start thinking, "We really need diversity around here."

That's certainly true in the Pacific Northwest in the United States, where people fleeing from California to Washington, Oregon, Idaho, and Montana are bringing the very attitudes that made their state unlivable. People look at them as rats bringing the plague with them, and it's not unreasonable.

So just to recap, I think a lot of people evade the long-term problem. A lot of people are unaware that there really is a long-term problem. They're too individualistic to want to band together and take responsibility for the problems their societies are facing.

They think that if they just go along and pay lip service to the multicultural regime—and maybe move to a better neighborhood—they can squeak through life with minimal problems. They're just not going to think or worry about the white people who are having acid thrown in their faces or being beaten and murdered by these invaders. So that's the general problem.

We really are a people with high individualism, low ethnocentrism, and low solidarity. We're very weak when faced with invaders who are highly ethnocentric, highly tribal, and have a dual ethical code, where they will treat their own people in one way and they will treat us in another way.

Basically, they are here to exploit us, and the best way of exploiting us is to exploit our white guilt and exploit our desire to be open, our feeling that it's high-minded to be open and not threatened by and not suspicious of strangers.

They're very good at exploiting those attitudes to their advantage. The trouble is there are so many of them, and their reproduction rates are sometimes twice as high as white Europeans, so eventually they're going to take over whatever country they're entering into.

Then there won't be an England anymore. There will still be a Pakistan for the Pakistanis. But there won't be an England for the English. That's not a future anybody should want.

White people love to be fair. So, in terms of fairness, what's fair about a world in which the only peoples that don't have homelands are the peoples of Europe? No Norway for the Norwegians. No England for the English. No France for the French. What you'll have instead are sprawling multicultural societies, primarily Islamic societies, that none of the former natives feel at home in. What's fair about that?

There's always going to be a Muslim world, full of Muslims. There's no shortage of them. There's no shortage of Chinese. There's no shortage of Indians. There's no shortage of Africans. In fact, there's a great abundance of them. There will always be an Africa for the Africans.

Why is it wrong for us to be concerned about keeping Europe for Europeans? Or America for Americans? Or Canada for Canadians? What's wrong with that? What's *unfair* about that?

TM: The other thing that a lot of people are very worried about—I'm concerned about as well—is when they hear ethnonationalists or White Nationalists saying, "We need our own space," they think, "Well, how are you going to achieve that? Is it going to involve death camps or genocide?" So how would you, for example, go about achieving such a thing in America or in Europe without doing a lot of harm?

GJ: Well, first of all, virtually everyone believes that you are justified in doing just about anything to avoid becoming a victim of genocide. That attitude has been drummed into us by six million Holocaust movies—that practically anything is justified if you're a victim of genocide.

Well, whites are facing a kind of genocide. Genocide doesn't have to be fast and hot and involve death camps and trenches full of corpses. It doesn't have to be that dramatic and photogenic.

The United Nations in the aftermath of the Second World War drafted a convention on genocide, which said that genocide also means the slow demographic erasure of distinct peoples. How does that happen? It can happen by invading their homeland and colonizing them and making it impossible for them to reproduce themselves.

That's what's going on in practically every white nation today with the exception of a few like Hungary and Poland that are trying to maintain their borders and ethnic integrity. Virtually every white nation is facing long-term prospects that are bleak. Even in Hungary and Poland, their reproduction rates are below replacement.

When you have a situation where more white people are dying than being born every year, eventually there will be no white people.

Why do we have this situation? It's not a mysterious cosmic inevitability. It's not a natural catastrophe. It's not a comet hitting the planet. It's the product of a culture and of a set of policies—political policies—that were enacted in the aftermath of the Second World War.

If whites are slowly facing extinction because of decisions that were made in the aftermath of the Second World War, then we can change those decisions. We can change those policies. We can alter our culture. We can change our values so that problem no longer exists.

The first thing we must do is simply to say: "No more immigration. Close the borders. It's over." Then the second thing is to start encouraging people to emigrate.

Even though whites are facing genocide as it's technically defined, in England or France or the United States, there are no death camps. Things look pretty good. Consumer electronics have never been cheaper. You've got more processing power in your smartphone than they did in the giant computers that sent men to the moon in the 1960s. "How are we facing genocide? It just doesn't seem to be happening." You can have a society that is generally pleasant and orderly, a society that has the appearance of being healthy and vibrant—vibrant in a good way, not in the euphemistic multicultural way—but where your long-term prospects are nil.

We should simply reverse these trends that are sending us in the wrong direction, that are sending us towards extinction. And we can do it as slowly and as stealthily as the genocide that's being enacted against us. We don't need a race war, a paroxysm of ethnic cleansing. We simply need to change the trends.

Just over fifty years ago the United States opened its borders to nonwhite immigration. We went from being a 90% white country to a 60% white country since then. I don't see any reason why we couldn't say, "Let's go back to the ethnic *status quo* of 1965."

Let's change our immigration policies. How would we do that? Well, first of all, no more immigration from the nonwhite world. Second, we start encouraging emigration by nonwhites. If it was possible for them to move here, it's possible for them to go back. If they came by planes, and trains, and automobiles, those things run both ways. It's possible for them to go back. It's not impossible; it's not inconceivable; it's simply a matter of will.

It's simply a matter of our instituting policies and trends that cause a net outflow of these people rather than a net influx. That's totally doable. People know how to do that.

So step one: We stop all immigration.

Step two: Everybody who's come here illegally—and that's a large number of them—you go over all of their paperwork with a magnifying glass. You find everyone that's made fraudulent applications for welfare, that has put in a fraudulent claim that he was being persecuted in his homeland, or whatever. You find these people and you deport them. They broke the law, so they've got no business here.

TM: Okay, so you're just talking about changing general trends and over time re-establishing white integrity of the country.

GJ: Yes, if it took fifty years for us to get into this mess, we can afford fifty years to get us out of this mess.

But here's the thing: let's say we embark upon a fifty-year project of returning America to the ethnic *status quo* of 1965. That was a great time in America in terms of productivity, in terms of national glory. It's when we had our space program going; fashion looked great; working-class incomes were probably as high as they had ever been. They started declining in the early 1970s. That was a great *status quo* year, when we were 90% white. If it took us fifty years to get back to that, that would be great.

But if we embarked on that program today, we'd start reaping the psychological benefits of it today. Because I think a great deal of the pathology of white people—the nihilism, the drug and alcohol abuse, the suicides, the alarmingly rising mortality of middle-aged working- and lower-class white people in the United States—is connected to the feeling that they've got no future. Not just as individuals, but as a group.

TM: Right, and they're not allowed to identify as part of a group. Psychologically it is actually very healthy to recognize your ethnic group and ancestors. I read recently that studying your genealogy and finding out about your ancestors improves your mental health and wellbeing. So you can only imagine what it's doing to us to be told we're not even allowed to feel any sense of pride or accomplishment for what our ancestors achieved.

GJ: But they will tell us that we should feel guilt for all the things that our ancestors did, right? I love that.

Well, wait a second, if it makes sense for us to feel collective guilt for things that other white people have done, then why is it wrong for us to feel collective pride for the things that other white people have done? When you look at the balance sheet, the things that we have to be proud of far outweigh the things we have to be ashamed of.

I really think it's not guilt so much as shame that's the issue. I don't feel any personal guilt for things that I don't do. I'm not responsible for things I don't do. But I can feel ashamed of the things that were done by my family or by my extended family, i.e., my racial family or my nation in the past. I can feel ashamed of that. But I can also feel pride for the good things that they've done.

And if white people started feeling pride for all the accomplishments of our people, we'd become much less tractable, and guilty, much less willing to be swindled out of our future.

So yes, I think you're right: a sense of who we are—a sense of rootedness, looking in the past, looking at previous generations and seeing your features and their faces—all of that is a very healthy experience.

I remember I was in Munich a few years ago. I went to the Wittelsbach palace, the Residenz Palace, and the best thing I saw there was the gallery of the ancestors. The Wittelsbachs created a gallery with portraits of all of their ancestors. Some of these, of course, were fanciful portraits, not from life, because their line went all the way back to the kings in the early Middle Ages from whom no portraits survive. For instance, Charlemagne was one of their ancestors.

It was fascinating to walk through this gallery and see all these faces. When they were actually portraits, you could see that, yes, these were the same people generation after generation after generation. Of course, European royals would marry their second and third cousins and so the same features would come back again and again and again. It was really a moving experience, a kind of sublime experience. I imagine it was especially that way for the actual Wittelsbachs who were viewing it. It was a reminder of who they are.

The greater the sense of rooted identity we have, the happier we're going to be, the prouder we're going to be, and the less easily swindled out of a future we're going to be.

But yes, there are going to be enormous psychological benefits to simply feeling that we have a future as a group again.

TM: A lot of people ask about the African Americans, who make up about 13% of the population. These people have lived there for multiple generations and speak English. Most of them haven't even been to Africa. You couldn't possibly expect them to repatriate to Africa after this stage. What would you say about that?

GJ: Well, first of all let me point out that is not a problem that you have to deal with in Great Britain. Or in France or in Norway.

TM: There are people who have been here for multiple generations, yeah.

GJ: Yeah, but there are two things here: They have even more multiple generations in previous homelands. The fact is that if their roots in those previous homelands didn't matter that much to them, why should their "roots," which are quite shallow, in your homeland matter all that much to you?

Also, we have a situation where people are constantly forced to move because of things like jobs, plants closing, or real estate becoming too expensive, so your neighborhood becomes unaffordable, your rents go up, or you have to move to search for a job because the factory that you worked in closed down and has reopened in Indonesia.

Nobody sheds a tear about people who are displaced because of private greed, private interests in the economic realm. So why should we be so broken up about the idea of people having to move for something that's really important, namely the common good of a people? I think that that is the kind of thinking we need to entertain.

Now as for blacks in America, yes, I think that the just and equitable solution for them would be to simply create a separate homeland for them in North America and encourage them to move there. Encourage them to move to several southern states and set up their autonomous homeland there.

You could just give them incentives to move there. Very significant numbers of blacks receive public assistance in the United States. Say, "Okay, you can collect your public assistance check in New Africa." I think that they'd up stakes and move there. Over time you'd get a situation where—again simply through gentle demographic pressures and incentives— the trend by which blacks emigrated from the South into the rest of the country, during and after the First World War, would be reversed. What were the reasons for that "Great Migration," as they call it? Jobs opened up. Whites were off fighting in Europe during the war.

TM: Okay, so you'd propose non-violent means using financial incentives and legal means such as deporting illegals to restore the original ethnic makeup of the United States and also European countries. I think that sounds very reasonable personally.

Of course, I suppose the main problem is that we've been so brainwashed to think that this is a hateful thing to do. What would your perspective be on how to counter this narrative that it's a hateful thing, based out of hate?

GJ: Well, first of all, hate is a natural, normal emotion that is sometimes defensible. It's simply true. Moreover, everybody hates somebody. So the only real question is: "Is it reasonable to feel hate in certain circumstances?"

Yes, you want to live in a society where there is a minimum of hatred and violence and tension between people of different ethnic groups. So how do you create that kind of society?

Well, as it turns out, ethnic hatred and tension are maximized by multiculturalism. So if we are really opposed to hatred and tension and ethnic violence, the best route is to reduce multiculturalism. Reduce it to an absolute zero if we can. That's really the best route.

I think it's perfectly natural, normal, and right to feel hatred in certain circumstances. And it's inevitable that there will be a lot of hatred—and not just hatred, but violence—in multicultural societies. So we need to decrease diversity, and that will decrease hatred.

Now you also have to ask about the people who are imposing these policies on us. I'm afraid that quite a lot of liberals and Leftists really do hate their own people. And aren't we being taught to hate ourselves, all this white guilt and multicultural propaganda?

So there's a whole lot of hate to go around here, and it's not all on us. The Left hate us. The Left hate their own societies. You can find plenty of statements where they will say, "I despise the English." Or, "What an evil corrupt society we are. We should hate ourselves." Entire generations are being taught to hate themselves.

TM: Yeah, absolutely, definitely. I've heard it so many times that "Oh, this town is too white" or "You know, this school is too white," is what I heard growing up.

Actually I'd also like to ask you a similar kind of question to the last one: What about mixed-race people? I know that sometimes people will say, "Well, what percentage white is acceptable?" Is it the one drop rule? What's going on here?

Or what about literally potentially dividing families, for example, with one black parent with one white parent? I know it's nitpicking, but what is your personal perspective or proposed policy regarding this?

GJ: Well, first of all, I'm a pragmatist about this. My attitude about race-mixing is that we should have a complete amnesty on past race-mixing, especially if it was in the distant past, but a complete moratorium on doing it in the future. We are thinking ahead, we are thinking about the future, so I would like there to be no more of it.

And then the question about what to do with people who are of mixed ancestry is really very simple. I think they should be encouraged to live with the people they are most comfortable with. If there's a white who married into a black family and has for all intents and purposes black children, I think that they should be encouraged to go with their family that they married into.

Now there are also differences between nonwhites. Some of them are more different from us than others. Blacks are very different from whites. I wouldn't call people from the Near East white or European, but they're certainly Caucasian. And honestly, I don't think that those people are a problem if there's a small admixture. In fact, there's been a small admixture of Near Eastern genes in many canonically European nations for a very long time. That doesn't really bother me.

With Asians, with Amerindians, with blacks, they're all different. Asians and Amerindians are less genetically distant from whites than blacks are. And so a small admixture of those populations doesn't really matter. And it really wouldn't matter at all if we were a growing population.

But the trouble is we are a shrinking population. And when you have a shrinking core population and you permit out-marriage, that's just hastening the day that we disappear as a distinct people. So I would support laws against miscegenation being instituted in the future.

But the best anti-miscegenation laws are simply having a

homeland. It's a passive anti-miscegenation law. It's like speed bumps. They're just there, so you've got to slow down. Borders are just there, so you don't end up meeting and marrying people who are racially different from yourself. That's really the best thing.

I remember being with a friend at the Metropolitan Museum of Art, and there was this white woman and her two daughters walking around the arms and armor collection, which is one of my favorite collections there. They were just so beautiful. And I said to my friend, "You know, there really needs to be a reservation where people like that can exist without being threatened." Then I said, "You know, it used to be called Europe."

TM: [laughter]

GJ: That was the white people reservation, right?

TM: Yeah, we need a reservation [laughter].

GJ: And how about Europe? Europe would be a nice reservation. So that's my attitude.

Honestly, having a small amount of nonwhite admixture would not be an issue if we had a growing white population. But we don't. We've got a declining white population, and therefore we can't really be lax about race-mixing into the future. We have to hold the line.

Now what would the attitude be in an America that is reconstituted on ethnic lines, toward people who have marginal African or Amerindian ancestry? Well, I think if they look white, think of themselves as white, and act white, and so forth, that they're white people for all intents and purposes, for all practical purposes.

However, if there are people within that society who want to remain genetically aloof from any admixture, that's fine. I would have no problem with that. But the whole purist thing would not be legislated but simply a matter of social customs and preferences that certain communities and families would have. I think that would be a reasonable and humane attitude.

TM: And I think that that ties in with the Jewish Question. What's your perspective on that, quickly?

GJ: The Jewish Question is basically this: First of all, Jews are a distinct people. They think of themselves as a distinct people. But there are Jews who in effect opt out of being Jewish by intermarrying with non-Jews and dropping their Jewish customs and religion and so forth. And that has happened a lot in the past, and my attitude towards people with marginal Jewish ancestry is basically this question, "Do you honor your Jewish ancestor's decision to opt out of the Jewish community? Or are you going to try to exploit that marginal Jewish ancestry to give yourself more credibility and power within the present system, which is largely Jewish dominated?" If they choose the former, then I don't have any problem with it, but if they choose the latter, then I'd start looking dimly upon them.

Jews are Caucasians. Middle Easterners are all Caucasians. Ashkenazi Jews are a mixture of people from the Near East and Europe. They're about 50/50. Honestly, if you've got a marginal Ashkenazi ancestry, that's a very small non-European percentage of DNA. And I just don't think it matters unless you make an issue of it. Unless you *make* it matter, right? You are as Jewish as you want to be, on that account.

However, as a rule, I would say let's have no more Jewish-Gentile admixture in the future. Let's try to separate ourselves. Let's keep our people distinct. I think that's a reasonable attitude. Again, amnesty for what happened in the past, as long as people don't make an issue of it, as long as they're not trying to identify with that group based on marginal ancestry. And a moratorium on it going forward.

TM: I guess the last remaining question, really, is how on Earth do we possibly convince the majority of the white population to even consider this idea?

GJ: We convince them by persuading them that it's necessary, first of all, that none of the other political options that are on the table are going to solve the basic problem that white people face: namely, long-term biological and cultural extinction. Conservatives aren't going to conserve us from that. Liberals are pushing it forward. We simply don't have any options. Libertarianism just hides our heads in the sand and pretends that it doesn't exist. There are no political options that will save us from long-term extinction, both as ethnic groups and as a biological race.

And once people get that through their thick heads and realize that it is possible to change this—it's only happened due to bad policies, most of which have been instituted in the last couple of generations—once they get it through their heads that it can be changed, and it can be changed in a way that's completely moral, then change will come.

TM: What about for people who say, "You know, I don't care what the world looks like in fifty years, I'm going to be gone anyway."

GJ: I think they're probably lying to you and to themselves. They really do care about it. But they've given up. They don't feel that they've got a future. They're afraid of fighting to have a future. So they're saying what does it matter anyway. So I think that on one level it's just a lie and a cop out.

They really do care. They just feel helpless. So we have to teach them that no, it's not hopeless. People can band together. They can change people's minds. They can change policies. And that's going to happen. It's already happening. The growth in what we're doing has been tremendous recently, and we will only continue. We don't need to have an absolute majority on our side. We just need a highly motivated, influential, and focused minority on our side.

And when I see the caliber—the intelligence, the creativity—of the people who are coming into this, and have come into this in the last couple years, we are gaining the ears of the best people of our race, the young ones, the people who have more future ahead of them and want to fight more for it. So I think things are actually looking up for us.

It's going to be a long, hard slog, there's no question about it. But given that nobody else has any solutions or even any inkling of what the problem is, and given that the Left is pretty tired and pretty hysterical now—now that Trump has happened, that Brexit has happened, and so forth—they're not attractive. Millennials and the next generation after them are noticing that the multicultural paradise is a lie. Their minds are open. So it's not hopeless. In fact, I'm very, very white-pilled about all of this. It's a great time for us to be alive. It's a glorious time.

I've always been skeptical of the "greatest generation" propaganda about the WWII generation. I always thought that was rubbish. Now I'm arguing that the millennials will be the greatest generation, because the millennials are going to be the ones who actually turn this whole thing around. The millennials are going to save our race and save our civilization. And the generation that's coming after them are going to do that as well. So you're the greatest generation. [laughter] You are coming over to our side. And this is a great time to be alive.

TM: Yeah, it's funny you say that, because obviously millennials are generally associated with some degeneracy and things like that, but we'll have to see how things turn out. Apparently Generation Z is fairly red-pilled on some things.

GJ: Z is not the last generation. I know Z is the last letter in the alphabet. No, no. Once you get to Z, then it starts over again.

TM: This is true.

GJ: And then Alpha after that, and a bright new future. So that's my outlook on this. I think that we are changing minds. Again, White Nationalism is really the only sober and responsible political position once you understand the situation that our race is in, demographically and politically. It's also a completely fair and humane and natural and normal reaction. And it doesn't have to be messy and sloppy and immoral and murderous. In fact, that's the future we're trying to avoid. We're trying to avoid a future of constant racial hatred and animosity.

We realize that there will never be a world without enemies. But there are ways of reducing conflict. The best way of reducing conflict is to give peoples with distinct ways of life, and distinct senses of identity and destiny, separate homelands where they can live without having to constantly fight against people on the bus, in their job, in the supermarket. It just gets so tiring. To step out your front door, in what used to be your homeland, and feel like you're jostling your way through an Arab *souk*.

TM: Which is exactly what I have to do every single time I leave the house. It's not very pleasant, I have to say.

Why do you call yourself a White Nationalist even though it's associated with the term "white supremacist," and people use it interchangeably? Do you think they are different, and aren't you worried about the connotations with that term? Because I actually do agree with you on 90% of what you said in this interview, but I wouldn't call myself a White Nationalist. Just because there are connotations that I wouldn't want to be associated with.

GJ: Right. We just have to change the connotations. That's my attitude. I wrote an article recently at *Counter-Currents* on this very issue: Are White Nationalists white supremacists?[1] And the answer is no, actually. We don't want to rule over other races. That's the whole point of being separate from them. We don't want to be ruled by them either. But we don't want to rule over them. We want to be separate.

The people who end up being white supremacists are the civic nationalist types, the Alt Lite types, the Gavin McInnes types, the people who say, "We're just going to surrender to all the demographic changes that have been made and imposed upon us since 1965; we're not going to change any of that; we're not going to stop it. We're not going to question it; we're just going to surrender to that. But we are going to be Western

---

[1] Greg Johnson, "Supremacism," *The White Nationalist Manifesto* (San Francisco: Counter-Currents, 2018).

cultural chauvinists."

Well, that boils down to enforcing white standards in a multiracial society. Enforcing, if you will, white supremacy. We've created a society where 40% of the population isn't white, but we're going to demand that they follow all the rules and mores and customs that are most comfortable for white people.

Now, of course the hat trick that they use to get out of that implication is to say that our values are universal. We're avatars of universal humanity. Like that line in *Full Metal Jacket*: "Inside every gook is an American trying to get out." And that's why we were in Vietnam. We were there to liberate them, not just from communism, but from their own culture, their own past, to allow them to be Americans. Because that's what they really want to be.

Well, that's not true. Different people really are different, and if they're really different, there are ways of life that are going to be more comfortable for them than the European way of life or the American way of life. That's why they're constantly demanding that we change the way that we live. They're trying to become more comfortable.

If we say, "You're here. We're not going to do anything about it. That would be politically incorrect even to consider it. But we're going to be Western chauvinists and defend the Western way of life, and you damn well better get used to it," that is *de facto* white supremacism. We are imposing white standards upon them. They might even find a token black who will go along with it. The token black in the Trump cabinet or the token black in the Proud Boys. But these people are seen by their own people as traitors.

TM: That's true. Absolutely. I'm sure we're all familiar with that situation of black people being called "white" just for wanting to go to school.

We've actually come up to an hour, so, thank you very much, Greg Johnson for joining me for this interview. If you guys want to find Greg Johnson's website it's Counter-Currents.com. Is there anything else you'd like our listeners to go and find from you, maybe books or social media?

GJ: My main presence is the *Counter-Currents* website that lists all of the books that we've published and all the books that we sell. There's new content five days a week. Sometimes two or three things a day. We have podcasts, we have articles, we have reviews. Occasionally a video.

It's a very important website. I think it's really the best intellectually oriented Anglophone White Nationalist website out there. If you haven't tried it, I'd encourage you to visit.

I want to thank you, Tara, for having me on the show. It's been a really enjoyable experience.

TM: Yeah, a great show and I hope all the listeners enjoyed it, and I'll catch you guys in the next video.

Counter-Currents, March 24, 2017

FROM METAPOLITICS TO HEGEMONY

INTERVIEW WITH
LANA LOKTEFF[*]

LANA LOKTEFF: Hello, ladies and gentlemen. My guest today, Greg Johnson, is the Editor-in-Chief of Counter-Currents Publishing and its journal and webzine, *North American New Right*. Greg, thanks for being here.

GREG JOHNSON: Thanks for having me on.

LL: Well, I regularly check in on and greatly enjoy your website *Counter-Currents*, and I am curious about your conversion into nationalism, so tell us how it happened for you.

GJ: Well, I went through a process, a long process—mostly based upon reading and observing things around me—from being a libertarian when I was an undergraduate student to becoming more conservative by the end of my undergraduate years. Then, when I went into graduate school, I was a conservative. I read a lot of neoconservative stuff. *The New Criterion* was one publication that I subscribed to. I subscribed to *Commentary* primarily because I liked the higher intellectual quality of the neocon writing. In terms of policies, I was more paleocon, I guess, but I liked the neocon writing. Never could stand *National Review*. Couldn't even look at it. It was such an ugly magazine. Stupid, too.

When I was in graduate school, I started realizing that, first of all, we're not just universal human beings, that we have specific ethnic identities. Of course, the liberal project and the libertarian

---

[*] This conversation took place in October of 2014. We would like to thank VS for making this transcript.

project is premised on the idea that there's just this universal humanity. We're these universal bearers of rights. We're basically fungible and interchangeable. Wherever we go, we're the same. That idea, I think, is fundamentally false. It goes along with the Enlightenment idea that ultimately we can settle everything by appeals to reason, by appeals to nature, whereas in the arena of politics you ultimately end up making an argument from *identity*.

In political debates you come back to a principle like this: This is just who I am. This is just what I'm comfortable with, and I can't budge. In other words, politics ultimately boils down to appeals to identity and being true to yourself. And since there are many different identities, many different groups, if you have non-negotiable appeals to identity, you're going to have conflict.

The idea of the Enlightenment is that we can resolve all conflicts because reason is one, and truth is one, and reality is one. So we can talk it all out and come to a consensus. But if in the realm of practical affairs you ultimately come back to appeals to identity, and identity is plural, that whole conflict resolution model is out the window.

Therefore, we are never going to live in a world where there's no enmity. The only way we're going to live in a peaceful world—or maximize the amount of peace in the world—is to allow different peoples with different identities to have their own spaces where they don't have to argue with others, where they don't have to convince others, where they can just live according to their identities, according to the way of life that feels natural to them.

This is true of individuals, too. Just have to share a bathroom with somebody, or have to share a bedroom with somebody, and you find that there's conflict. But that conflict can be easily removed if you just don't have to share certain spaces.

I think it was Virginia Woolf who talked about how there would be just as many great women writers as men writers if they only had a room of their own to go to.

Nationalism is basically the idea that we should all have a country of our own to go to. A place where we can retreat and be ourselves and not be on trial by the standards of universal reason or by the different standards of our neighbors, but where we can simply relax and be at home and be ourselves.

So, I became a nationalist when I realized that there are certain irreducible differences between people, and that those have to be respected and honored, and that's the only route to a world that's going to be as close to utopia as possible, where everybody has a country of his own.

LL: Well said. I read your book, *New Right vs. Old Right*, which for me was a lot of fun, but for those just hearing about the New Right, what is new about the North American New Right and how does it differ from the Old Right and the European New Right?

GJ: These are good questions. First of all, in the 1970s some French journalists labeled Alain de Benoist as an exponent of something called the "New Right." He's never been comfortable with that term. His followers have never been comfortable with that term. They always clear their throats and announce that they're not comfortable with that term, and that this is a term that other people have placed upon them.

Personally, I'm just going to claim that term.[1] I'm following Jonathan Bowden in this. He claimed the term "New Right." I think it's a fine term, because, first of all, it's meaningful to talk about being Right-wing. What's essential about the Right is that we believe that human inequality is not always a bad thing. The Left is elitist in practice, but in terms of their principles, in terms of their values, they are anti-elitist. They're egalitarian. I think that is an essential difference between Left and Right.

In many of my policy views, in many of my lifestyle choices, in the kinds of people I hang out with, in the kinds of coffee houses and neighborhoods I go to, I'm pretty liberal. However, in terms of my basic value orientation I am a Rightist, because I believe that inequality is natural, normal, and not necessarily bad.

---

[1] Greg Johnson, "New Right vs. Old Right," *New Right vs. Old Right* (San Francisco: Counter-Currents, 2013).

Now, what's the difference between the New Right and the Old Right? I think that, really, you have to talk about the difference between the New Left and the Old Left in order to understand that. The Old Left was totalitarian. It was militant. It was imperialistic. It was certainly genocidal. We're talking about classical Communism.

After the Second World War, something emerged called the New Left. First it was called Western Marxism, but then the "New Left" was the term that was used beginning in the 1960s. It was an alternative to the totalitarian political model. Basically, it aimed to advance the values of the Left through different means. Instead of battles in the streets or on battlefields in the Old Left style, they took a page from Antonio Gramsci, the Italian Marxist, and talked about attaining hegemony in culture.

Classical Marxism claims that culture is an epiphenomenon of economics and politics. Therefore, to change the culture you change the political and economic sublevel of society. Whereas Gramsci said no, we can actually change politics by changing culture, by changing the way people think and perceive the world.

The New Left has created this strange phenomenon that we have today of a Left-wing capitalist oligarchical society. We have a hyper-oligarchical capitalist society. And yet all of its reigning values are Leftist, because the Left, particularly after the Second World War, put a huge amount of its emphasis on changing culture, changing ideas. And they have achieved a kind of cultural hegemony.[2]

I think that the New Right needs to take a page from the New Left. We need to reconfigure our project so that we're not imitating Old Right models anymore. A lot of people on the Right today really do have Old Right models. They want to have a uniformed, militant political party that's centralized, has a leadership principle, and aims to create a totalitarian society.

We need to deconstruct the existing intellectual and cultural hegemony of the Left through intellectual and cultural means. Then we need to construct a new hegemony, a Rightist hegemo-

---

[2] Greg Johnson, "Hegemony," *New Right vs. Old Right*.

ny that makes the preservation of our race a non-negotiable political principle across the whole political spectrum. That's the aim, as I conceive of it, of the New Right.

Now, I have to say something: The Old Right was totally legitimate in the tactics that they chose. I can't endorse everything they did, because you can't endorse everything that happens in a war. But tactically it was totally legitimate for Hitler and Mussolini to choose paramilitary organizations, centralization, and a militant kind of totalitarian one-party politics. Why? Because that is what they were fighting against.

They were fighting against Communism, and Communism was one of the great dangers that our civilization has faced, the greatest danger since the Muslim invasions and the Mongols and the Huns. Communism is one of the worst things that ever happened in human history. They had to fight it, and they had to fight it using its own means, because liberal democracy was not up to the task. So, that said, I think it was totally legitimate for them to adopt the strategies, the tactics, of their enemies in order to defeat them.

However, the enemy has adopted new strategies and tactics, and we need to be just as supple and flexible. We need to keep our aims the same, and I do think the aims of the New Right are basically the same as the Old Right. We want some kind of organic society that's ethnically defined. But at the same time we need to change our means of getting there in order to effectively combat the way that we are actually being ruled, which is not through a hard totalitarianism but through a kind of soft, intellectual, totalitarian hegemony that the Left has created in our culture today.

LL: Now, if you boil down the message of the North American New Right, what would it be?

GJ: That's a good question, and basically what I say we stand for is "truth, justice, and a nice white country."[3] That's what we

---

[3] Greg Johnson, "Introduction: Truth, Justice, and a Nice White Country," *Truth, Justice, & a Nice White Country*.

want. The enemy stands for lies and injustice and multiculturalism. They stand for mixing it all up and making a pigsty of every white country that exists.

Political correctness, which is the face of the Left today, boils down to a kind of moralistic drama of lying. Political correctness has two aspects: one, false excuses for privileged groups, and two, false accusations of blame directed at us, at white people. That is lying. That is injustice. We stand for truth and justice.

We're going to tell the truth about race. We're going to tell the truth about identity. We're going to tell the truth about what makes a society work.

Justice for us means treating people appropriately given their nature. It's just to treat equal people equally. It's unjust to treat unequal people equally. Since all people are different, our view of justice basically boils down to treating people appropriately, and that is going to create a hierarchical society. Some people are going to have more: They're going to have more things; they're going to have more responsibility; they're going to have more fame and acclaim. Others are going to have less. But we're going to make sure that different outcomes are proportionate to real differences in their natures. It's not just based on birth or wealth and things like that.

The third principle, the nice white country, well, that's the aim. We want to create an ethnostate. We want to create a lot of ethnostates. By ethnostates, I mean, basically, sovereign entities where distinct ethnic groups have their own country. That means Swedes, but it also means the Piedmontese; it means the Sicilians. There are lots of different ethnic groups that don't have their own countries today. I was a big supporter of Scottish independence, and I'd love to see Wales become independent, too, if they prefer that. Again, I think the best solution for ethnic conflict, and the best way to create conditions of peace and progress, is to create separate homelands for all the different, distinct white ethnic groups.

In the United States, different European ethnic groups have blended into a new people. I hope the United States will break up into regions, probably along existing jurisdictions, along state boundaries, or sub-boundaries within states. So, there might be many different white areas in North America. I think that would be a good thing.

Again, we stand for truth, justice, and a nice white country. Lots of nice white countries. To gain that we believe that we're going to have to redraw borders, and we're going to have to move populations around.

I think that one of the worst betrayals of Nick Griffin in the British National Party was to give up the idea of repatriating nonwhites from England. These people have no business being there. Absolutely no business whatsoever. And if it was feasible for these people to be brought there in the millions, it's feasible for them to leave in the millions. There's nothing that stands in the way of doing that except the political will and courage to do it, and it could be done in a completely humane fashion.[4] It doesn't even need to be a giant government program. Most of these people came under their own volition. They can leave under their own volition once we make clear that this is what we want and once we create incentives for that to happen. So, again, a nice white country is going to require changing boundaries, and it's going to require moving populations

But we think it's worth it, because ultimately if we don't have White Nationalism our race is going to become extinct.[5] The white race is on the path to extinction right now. If current trends continue there will be no white people in the world, and the only way to really prevent white extinction is for us to have our own sovereign homelands.

LL: Now, some people will say, "Uh oh, isn't this Fascism or National Socialism?" so how would you distinguish the difference here?

GJ: First of all, I'm not going to just say, "Oh, no. We're not like those horrible people!" We *are* like those people, and I don't

---

[4] Greg Johnson, "Restoring White Homelands," *The White Nationalist Manifesto*.

[5] Greg Johnson, "White Extinction," *The White Nationalist Manifesto*.

think they're entirely horrible. I can't endorse everything they did, of course, but I think Fascism and National Socialism were legitimate responses to their time, and that they also contained within them things of permanent value.

At the core of them is the idea of restoring a kind of organic, hierarchical society in the context of modernity, and I think that is a reasonable goal. There is a critique of capitalism; there's a critique of liberalism; there's a critique of internationalism and globalization. All of those things are completely valid, and I want to maintain those. I want to maintain their concern with race; the German National Socialists, specifically, were very concerned with that. The Italians sort of lagged behind. I want to preserve their absolutely important concern with identifying the Jewish question, the Jewish problem. That has to be kept fully in mind. So, there's a lot about these people that I agree with and I want to preserve.

What's the difference? Well, like I said, I think at the time when they were fighting against totalitarian, imperialist, and genocidal Communism they adopted appropriate countermeasures. They took a gun to a gun fight. Today, we are ruled not by hard totalitarian Leftism. We're ruled by a kind of soft totalitarian cultural and intellectual hegemony, and instead of taking a gun to a battle of ideas we need to take ideas to a battle of ideas. So, that's really the difference.

What is the outcome as I view it? My view is this: We live in a society where we have tremendous choices, and people feel quite free. The average person feels free. You and I don't feel free because we see the strings, right? The average person feels quite free. They have all kinds of trivial options to choose from in toothpaste, in politics, and so forth.

At the core of the Left is the organized Jewish community. When I talk about Left-wing domination, I really am talking about Jewish domination, Jewish hegemony. They're the key, the core to the Left, and they always have been. What we have in America today is a range of political options, but every one of those political options is carefully vetted so that it's safe for Jews, and it's conducive to Jewish interests.

Now, I don't see any reason to change the basic system of

having lots of choices. I just want to make sure that once the New Right attains power, all the political choices that people have available to them are safe for whites. White genocide, white extinction, white degradation are going to be off the table and no longer options for anybody up and down the political spectrum. You simply won't be able to choose that, just like you can't choose anything that endangers Jewish interests today. I think that whites in white countries should be as sacrosanct as Jews are today. That's basically the end point.

So, what would it look like? Well, it would look a lot like today if I had my druthers. There'd be lots of choices. There'd be pluralism in politics. But behind the scenes, there would be a consensus that vets every political candidate, that would be working to create a culture that would be conducive to white interests.

There would be lots of differences. Whites would still be arguing about abortion and taxes and feminism and so forth. But it would just be an argument within the family. We would have family differences, and there would be no option of bringing in outsiders as allies to gain advantages over members of our own extended family. So, that's the end game as I conceive of it.

Not such a scary prospect, because liberals today consent to live under that system. It's just that it's a system rigged to destroy them and their values and all the rest of us. I just want to get rid of that rigging, so to speak. I want to get rid of the anti-white bias and the pro-Jewish bias and switch the system around so it preserves and enhances our interests.

LL: Yeah, you talk about why you think it's important for White Nationalists to adopt an elitist strategy and you also talk about directing the message to the educated, the professional classes and above, to mold the masses. Can you talk about that?

GJ: First of all, I don't want to carry around the banner of elitism primarily. I think that is something of a mistake. It's necessary. You have to say it in some contexts. But we're never going to have a political movement that is potent if we go around saying, "We're elitists! Vote for us! Vote for the few!" It's never going to happen, because most people are going to look at that and they're going to say, "What's in your elitism for me?"

My attitude about elitism is that it is an inevitable consequence of justice. And there's something in justice for everybody. So, this is why I say "truth, justice, and a nice white country." Justice is something that everybody wants. Unless you're bad, and then you don't want to get what you deserve, right? But most people want to be treated justly.

But, as William Blake says, "One law for the ox and the lion is injustice." So, we need laws that treat equal people equally and unequal people unequally. Aristotle called this proportional equality. The idea is that people should be unequal proportionate to their real worth. That's the model that we want, and that means that there will be people who have more responsibility, more fame, etc. based on their worth. I think that's important to bear in mind. What we stand for is justice, but justice will lead to hierarchy in society, and we want to make sure that is a *just* hierarchy, rather than the unjust kind of hierarchies that exist today. Even though we have a society that's constantly paying lip service to equality, it's a very stratified and very unjust society.

So, where does elitism come in in terms of our strategy? Well, we have to recognize that for the most part history is made by minorities. Most people don't have the time or the understanding or the education to have an impact on society. Most people are just dragged along by the few, by the elites. That's always been the case. The best sort of situation for a people is to have an elite that is organically connected to them and that looks out for their interests.

I wrote a piece for *Counter-Currents* called "Notes on Populism, Elitism, and Democracy."[6] What I make clear in there is that I'm a populist in the sense that I believe the only legitimate political system looks out for the interests of all the people. However, I also argue that the political system that best looks out for the interests of all people is going to be one where leadership is on average better than the masses.

---

[6] Greg Johnson, "Notes on Populism, Elitism, and Democracy," *New Right vs. Old Right*.

Most people understand that instinctively. We want our leaders to be better than us on average, just as we want our doctors to know more about medicine than we do, and our dentists to know more about teeth than we do, and the guy who sets up our new TV to know more about TVs than we do. We recognize that expertise gives authority, and we want that in politics as in every other area of life.

Yet at the same time we want these experts to be responsive to the interests of the whole. So, that's my idea. I think we have to be populist in the sense that we look out for the interests of everybody, elitist in the sense that we recognize that the best way to do that is to have people who are on average smarter and more public-spirited in positions of authority.

To get that, we need to create that elite. Our race is leaderless. There's nobody looking out for the interests of white people. The people who run our societies are looking out for the interests of Jews. They're looking out for the interests of themselves. They're looking out for the interests of the rich. Nobody's looking out for the interests of whites. If we are going to have a society where white interests are sacrosanct we are going to need a leadership caste that looks out for white interests. And the only way to get that is to start appealing to people today who are better than average in terms of intelligence, morality, public-spiritedness, taste, and so forth, to try to create the leadership caste that we are going to need down the road.

My approach is basically to search all existing social classes, all existing white constituencies. I'm spreading a very broad net. I want to find the best white people for the cause, and I want to persuade the best white people of my vision of things and to get them writing, thinking, organizing, and becoming that organically connected elite that will provide the leadership caste for our race. Because eventually we are going to have to take control politically of our own destiny again, and to do that we must have the leadership. That's my goal. That's why I have an elitist focus.

By an elitist focus I do not mean that I am just appealing to the educated. I'm trying to appeal to the *best* people in all political classes, in all social classes, in all levels of education. There are lots of really bright people who've never been to college, and in fact some of the brightest people I know are largely self-educated. So, I'm not a snob in the social class sense of the term, although I do recognize that people with better educations and more money do have more power in society. But I am a snob in the sense that I want to find the best people no matter where they are in the current social system, and I want to bring them into my vision of things, because I do think we need a leadership caste that will actually take the interests of our race into account.

LL: Now, you also write about the need to focus on metapolitics and you compare it to occult warfare and the points you talk about are (1) propaganda and (2) community organizing.[7] Can you talk about this?

GJ: Metapolitics is just a term that refers to the things that have to be established for there to be political change. Basically I break metapolitics down into two categories. One is the battle of ideas, propaganda basically, and two is community organizing.

There are certain ideas that need to be established in people's minds if we're going to live in a White Nationalist society. We have to get people concerned with the danger to our race. We have to awaken people to the fact that there are bigger problems than abortion and school prayer and what's going on in the Middle East. Namely, our race is becoming extinct. It's that dire, and we need to be as worried about white extinction as some people are worried about Bengal tigers and snail darters and rare frogs that are going extinct as well. We're going to be extinct. And when the white race goes extinct, all those other species are going to go extinct too, because we're the only ones who really care about preserving them. So, we need to awaken people to the danger.

We need to awaken people to their identity. We need to get white people to think of themselves *as* white people, and to think of themselves as white people *unapologetically*. So, there's a

---

[7] Greg Johnson, "Metapolitics and Occult Warfare," *New Right vs. Old Right*.

moral element to this, too. We have to teach people that it's not only normal to belong to a group, but it's also right to take your group's side in conflicts. White people have had that notion bred out of them, and we need to start taking our own side, because we do live in a world of ethnic conflicts.

We also need to have ideas about what's feasible. Nobody's going to accept the idea of the white ethnostate if they think that it's simply impossible to create. So we have to convince people that it is possible.

These are metapolitical ideas that need to be argued out and established, and they need to be propagated to all white groups, and we need to have ways of propagating these things and making them appealing to every white constituency, every white age group, every white ethnic group, every white nation, and so forth. That's the intellectual aspect of metapolitics.

LL: And that's why political diversity among pro-whites can also be a good thing, right?

GJ: Whites are a diverse group, and pro-whites are going to need to be able to speak to all different groups. So the more diversity among pro-whites, the more ways that we have of matching up with the existing diversity of white groups, so it helps us. We should embrace that. That's a strength. It really is a strength.

Now, the community organizing aspect of metapolitics is basically the idea that it's got to be more than just ideas. We need existing communities among white people. I'm not talking about political parties. That's politics proper. I'm talking about metapolitics. I'm just talking about real world networks, families, extended families, tribes, mutual aid networks, businesses, and things like that. We have to think in terms of taking it off the internet, geographically localizing, and building real communities. So, that's the second part of metapolitics.

My focus is on those two things. Mostly on the battle of ideas, because I'm just one guy out here on the internet, so that's primarily what I can do. However, one of the things that I try to do in the community organizing field is to bring together people I know of who are in the same area but who might not know one another, and get them to meet one another, and try to foster face-to-face interactions amongst our readers.

Counter-Currents is a node. I have all this information going out, and I have all these people checking in. When people check in they say, "Hey, I like your work. Here's a donation. Here's a book order." I look at the address, and I say, "Wait a second here. I know another guy in the same little town in Florida that you're in right now. Do you want to meet?" and they say, "Yeah, sure!" So, I put these people in touch, and suddenly two very lonely dissidents have somebody that they can meet for coffee.

LL: Yeah, that's great.

GJ: It's a small beginning, but, you know, the longest journey begins with a single step. Also, I go around and make occasional talks. I meet people in the real world. I used to have dinners, and at these dinners I discovered that there were a couple of people in the same town, but they didn't know each other in the real world, so I made sure that everybody in the room raised their hands and said what town they're from. I said, "Hey! You two are from Petaluma! You better get together after the talk and exchange cards." So, I've done that kind of stuff. I'd like to do more of it, but, you know, there are only so many hours in the day.

So, those are two areas that I am focused on, and I'm hoping that if the metapolitical foundations are strong, then somebody's going to come along with the right combination of political skills and charisma, at the right time politically, and suddenly it's going to be possible for a really effective political movement to just gel. But until those metapolitical foundations are in place, there's going to be a lot of headwind against it. It's going to be very thin and AstroTurfy. There's going to be no grassroots basis for it, because there's no real grassroots white community, no conscious white community. Most of our people are unconscious, and we have to change that.

LL: Well, some people claim that the genocide of Europeans is something we did to ourselves, and I know you strongly oppose this. So, to what extent is white dispossession our fault?[8]

GJ: Well, once we are fully aware of the problem and we choose to do nothing, I think then we become part of the problem. However, most people are not responsible for what's happened to them. Again, politics is something that is created by elites, and it's *done to* most people. White dispossession is being *done to* white people, and I strongly oppose this rather grandiose idea that, "We're doing it to ourselves! Our race is committing suicide!" It's not true. Our race is not committing suicide. Some people are doing this to the rest of us.

Who are those people? Well, they're disproportionately Jews. They're not even whites. So, it's my view that it's closer to the truth to say whites are being murdered, and the people who are putting in place the trends that are leading to white dispossession and white extinction are disproportionately Jewish, and that Jews are not only disproportionately responsible for setting up this system, they are the main impediment to changing it. And I think that's an important distinction.

A lot of whites will get sidetracked, basically, arguing about what percentage of our problems are caused by Jews as opposed to Christianity or capitalism or whatever. It's an argument about whether we're doing it to ourselves or whether it's being done to us. Arguing that point can be sterile. We can do that forever.

Ultimately though, we are not a debating society. We're not here to establish merely historical points. We're here to change the future. And when you talk about changing the future, when you talk about changing the existing trends that are destroying our race, ask yourself, "Who's standing in the way?" It's the organized Jewish community. They are the linchpin of resistance to every sensible policy to halt white extinction, white dispossession. So, when you start thinking politically and you start thinking about who winds up against us, it's the Jews.

They're not the sole group. They're very small in number. They're very powerful, and they have power because they're

---

[8] Greg Johnson, "Our Fault?," *New Right vs. Old Right*.

good at making coalitions. So, the Jews are the core of this minority/disgruntled coalition, which of course is the majority of humanity when you start incorporating all nonwhites into it. But within white societies they organize nonwhite minorities, they organize gays and lesbians, they organize environmentalists. Anybody on the Left, they try to organize and make part of their coalition in order to project power.

Yet, at the same time, when you look at which policies dominate, it's the Jewish agenda of white race replacement that always dominates. So, for instance, feminists always fall silent when anybody brings up the problem of rape. Because when you look at rape in Scandinavia it's not Scandinavian men who are raping women at levels that you find in a war zone, it's nonwhite immigrants. And yet, where are the feminists opposing this? There are no candlelight marches against Islamization. They are silent, because the feminist agenda is always trumped by the Jewish anti-white race replacement agenda.

We need to break up the coalition of the Left by making clear that these non-Jewish groups on the Left, that are part of the Leftist coalition, will never get their way whenever their values conflict with white race replacement. It's true of gays and lesbians. It's true of feminists. It's true of environmentalists. All these groups routinely get steamrolled whenever there's a chance to bring in more diversity.

LL: Well, on that note, is Judeo-Christianity compatible with White Nationalism?

GJ: Well, when you put the "Judeo-" in there it sort of prejudices me.

LL: Yeah, because I know there are a lot of nationalists . . . You know, the Christian versus pagan argument.

GJ: I think that's an important discussion to have. I think that the value system of Christianity is incompatible with White Nationalism. I think that if you look at the suicidal values, if you will, that a lot of whites do have programmed into them, they are justified in terms of Christian doctrine, Christian attitudes, and we'd be better off weaning these people away from these attitudes. When you start talking about the necessity of taking our own side in ethnic conflicts, the first thing a lot of people will say is, "Well, that goes against my Christian values. Turning the other cheek and things like that." It's a problem. It's definitely a problem. So, I think we need to have a mature discussion of this within our ranks.

I'm not a Christian. I've never been a Christian in the sense that I believed in the Christian value system, and I think that it's a weakness in our race. It's one of the weaknesses that has allowed Jews so much power over us. Because of course if you believe the New Testament then the Jews have a particularly important place in the history of mankind, specifically the sacred history of mankind, and that has given them a great deal of power over us for one thing.

So, my tendency is to think that Christianity is one of the weaknesses in our society, and I think that as whites become less influenced by Christianity, maybe that is going to open up the possibility of being less sheep-like and weak in the face of our impending genocide. That's my hope.

LL: Well, another weakness we have and you talk about it in a chapter called "The Perils of Positive Thinking."[9] Ultimately, you say, it cannot save our people. Can you talk about this?

GJ: "The Perils of Positive Thinking" piece relates to the "blame ourselves" meme. I definitely think that people who want to keep it all positive and people who want to not go populist and not talk about reasons for white people to feel resentment and anger are on the wrong track. Our race is being destroyed. We have every reason to be righteously resentful and angry about that. The people who say, "Keep it positive!" are sort of delusional. It's like sticking daisies in the rifles of soldiers. It's not a very effective counter-measure. Talk about taking a

---

[9] Greg Johnson, "The Perils of Positive Thinking," *New Right vs. Old Right*.

knife to a gunfight, how about taking a daisy to a gunfight? It's sort of a hippy-dippy non-starter.

I think that being negative and being depressed is a bad thing. I am a fundamentally optimistic person in terms of the struggle. But I think that the people who say we've got to keep it all positive are wrong. We need to fully embrace and understand the horror that's being committed against us, and we need to fully mobilize the righteous indignation that white dispossession and white extinction should be causing.

LL: Yep. Would you say that we're still in the early stages of formulating the foundations for a white republic?

GJ: Yes and no. I think the basic ideas are there. I don't think that we need to worry too much about what legal system we'll have and will there be two houses of parliament or one or anything like that. All of that stuff has been done, basically. Whites have come up with brilliant systems of government for thousands of years. It's in our genes. We've got that handled. As soon as white people put our minds to it and get serious about it, the political stuff will simply take care of itself.

What we're in the early stage of is convincing people of the *necessity* of doing that. So, drawing blueprints and designing flags and uniforms is all premature. All that will take care of itself, and a lot of that stuff has been taken care of by the rich political tradition that whites already have. The United States constitution, you could spruce that up a little bit and it would be just fine. I honestly think so.

But we're just at the beginning stages of getting people to realize the necessity of reorienting politics away from the center-Left vs. center-Right bickering about things that don't really matter, towards preserving our race. Once people get their minds wrapped around the danger and the necessity of moving towards a white republic, politics will take care of itself. But we're just at the beginning of that journey.

LL: What could you say to willing, intelligent folks who are passionate about this cause, but don't know what they can do?

GJ: It depends on where they are in their lives, what they have going for them, if they're just starting out, if they're well established, if they have a lot of independence, or if they're very dependent on others for their livelihood. So, there are a lot of different options. I guess the first thing I would say to anybody is just get educated about these things and get passionate about them. Second, take stock of your life and determine what you're willing to give up, what you're willing to spend, and therefore what you can do within those parameters.

I think it's very important for you to meet other people in your area who share these views, but you've got to be really careful because, you know, some of the best people I know are White Nationalists, and some of the worst people I've ever encountered are White Nationalists. You've got to be a little careful about who you meet. Don't invite people to your house that you've never met before. That can be a very big mistake. People on the Left are very careful about that. They always pick neutral places to meet people. They don't invite somebody they've never met to their houses. So, we need to be smart about things like that.

So, get educated and start making connections with like-minded people in your area. Those are the first things that you could do. After that, the direction you go depends on where you are in your life, what your resources are, etc. If you're retired, if you're quite comfortable, you might consider becoming a more open advocate. If you're just a college student starting out in life, you don't want to go through life with a big cloud of controversy over your head, you might want to think about being a secret agent rather than a public standard bearer.

The point that I try to make in *New Right vs. Old Right* and my other writings is that we must be willing to accept a whole range of different white options. We have to allow every white person who's racially conscious to determine his or her own level of explicitness and involvement. We're not going to be chewing them out and saying, "You coward!" I don't know why certain people make the decisions they make. Especially people I've never met. I'm not going to question their decisions. I will try to persuade everybody to expand their comfort zones. I'm constantly trying to persuade people to do more. But I respect people who keep it on the down low, so to speak, who want to be secret agents.

We need people like that, because if every person who believes what we believe suddenly decided on National Coming Out as a White Nationalist Day to out themselves, well, the system would have them in its beams, and a lot of these people would be scarred and jobless and friendless and be harmed by it. And that would only make the system stronger and the movement weaker. I don't want that to happen.

LL: Stay in the nationalist closet!

GJ: Some people need to. And we need to respect those decisions. Other people who can afford to be out there, they should be out there. I want there to be more explicit White Nationalists. I want there to be people in every community who are known as White Nationalists.

I talked to Robert Taylor of the band Changes recently. He talked about his own activism. He said one of the most important things for any activist to do is sell yourself as a person before you can sell your message, your program. I think that's a very important thing for people to contemplate, because if you're living in a community and you're not very well known in that community and suddenly you become an explicit White Nationalist, you're going to become the local crank. Because a lot of people are not going to know who you are. They're only going to know you as somebody who has aberrant, radical political views. That's probably not a good way of going about it. You're not going to do much for the cause, and you're not going to do much for yourself. You're eventually going to get alienated and burned out, and we don't want that. We want for people to stick with this in the long haul.

So, what do you do if you want to become the local White Nationalist? Well, first of all, it's important for people to know who you are *without* the politics, *before* the politics. It's important to be a good dad and a good Little League coach, a member of various community groups, the guy who's involved with the art show. Anything that makes you a public, known figure and sells you as an individual.

If you are a well-established member of a community, if people like you for who you are, if people know that you are responsible, public-spirited, altruistic, and trustworthy, then, when it comes out that you have some kind of aberrant political views, it's not going to hurt you as much. In fact, by being a stand-up guy and a member of the community it's actually going to positively advertise those views.

So, make yourself as good a person as possible, as an individual and as a member of the community. Be as well-liked and likeable as possible. Be involved. If it's animal rights or organizing a farmers' market or whatever, be involved. Sell yourself as an individual. Be a person who's trusted. And when your ideas come out, or when you decide to talk about your ideas, you're going to have some authority. That's going to cushion the blow. You might find yourself in a very strong position to actually change people's minds. Sell yourself before you sell your ideas. Establish yourself before you start establishing your ideas. I think that's very wise advice.

LL: Yeah, it reminds me of Kai Murros. He's right. I hate to say it, but in today's world you have to be well-packaged and also sell the idea culturally. Nationalism has to look cool. People have to want to be a part of it. Unfortunately, that's how it is.

GJ: That's true. And isn't it always better to be cool anyway? Jonathan Bowden talks about that too.

Part of the appeal of our ideas is that they are a little out there. Our ideal advocates are respectable and well-established in their communities. But they've got something a little extra, even something a little dangerous about them. That's also very appealing.

You don't want to be totally out there. You don't want to be some guy with long stringy hair and a sandwich board standing in the park baying about the end of the world. That just makes you the local crank. But if you're totally indistinguishable from any other milquetoast Rotarian, that's not a good thing either. So, you've got to be the well-respected local guy with a quality of idealism, a visionary quality that sets you apart and attracts others to you. That's a hard balance to strike, but it is ideal.

LL: Well, I really see the new counter-cultures coming out, and it's young nationalists I see. You know, good-looking, well-dressed. They're fun; they're trendsetters; they have an edge. I think we're going to see a lot of that coming out probably even in the next ten years.

GJ: I totally agree. I think the trend that I've seen since I've gotten involved with this . . . I've been really involved with this since 2000. The trend has been that every year it seems the average age of people involved is younger, the average education level is a little higher, the sex ratio is a little more balanced. When I got started I was frequently the youngest person in a room of grey-headed men. Now, it's a room with 30% women or 40% women in some groups and the average age of people is under forty.

That's a huge change, and that's a change that really makes me hopeful, because you need to be able to look and *see* the future of our cause. When the cause is over sixty on average, it doesn't have much future, but younger people have more future in them. So, when I see younger people who are really together involved in this, it's just encouraging. It's a concrete proof that our race has a little bit more of a future than it did just a few years ago.

We strive to represent the interests of all white people. Whites as a race do not have a future right now. And we have to bear in mind—the back of our minds, perhaps—that not all whites will have a future. We can't save everyone. We might be becoming a new race, the whites who have a future.

That's what I see when I go to these gatherings now. When I went to the London Forum meeting back in September it was a very impressive group of people. I really felt these are white people with a future. It might not be the whole race, but there is a group of whites forming now that do have a future, and that's very encouraging.

LL: As we end the hour, please share any closing remarks for us.

GJ: Please visit *Counter-Currents*. I'm prejudiced, but I think it's the best English language, Right-wing, New Right webzine out there.

LL: I would agree.

GJ: We try to publish new material every weekday. A number of days we have multiple new things on the website. It's a growing community. It's a growing movement. It's getting younger and smarter and cooler and more effective. Every day I get up I feel new concrete reasons to be hopeful for the future. So, I really want to thank you for all the work you're doing at Red Ice Radio. I think you're part of this rising tide, and I really appreciate the chance to be on your show.

LL: Thank you so much.

Counter-Currents, November 3, 2014

Destigmatizing Racism

A Conversation with
Hugh MacDonald*

GREG JOHNSON: I'm Greg Johnson. Welcome to *Counter-Currents Radio*. Today I am going to have a conversation with Canadian film-maker Hugh MacDonald. He is doing some work on an essay presentation that he is going to be giving in London next month. He wanted to bounce some ideas off of me, and we thought it prudent to record it in case other people would find it beneficial as well. So, Hugh, welcome to the show.

HUGH MACDONALD: Thank you.

GJ: What's on your mind? What are you working on exactly? And how can I help you?

HM: I am trying to do a study of the concept of racism. One aspect is to come up with a response to when people call you racist. But more broadly it's just to try to understand what does racism really mean. What is this concept? And does it have any validity? I am trying to look it this idea within the context of feminist argument of "slut-shaming." I am trying to apply the technology of this feminist argument to racism. And I am calling it "racism-shaming."

GJ: Right. So, what's the feminist position on slut-shaming in a nutshell?

HM: There is something called the "slut walk," which is a feminist protest movement. It is designed to push against the idea of "slut shaming." This idea of "slut walk" was first began in my university (York University, Toronto) when a cop came to campus and said that in order to avoid rape, make sure you

---

* This is *Counter-Currents Radio* podcast that was recorded in March 2015. I want to thank Mahometus for the transcript.

don't dress like a slut. Feminists don't like that argument because in telling women to not dress like a slut or to not be a slut we are controlling their behavior. From their perspective, we are infringing on their autonomy. According to them, women should be free to do whatever they want to do, and they shouldn't have men telling them what to do. That is what feminism is all about. Probably one big aspect of a certain type of feminism is this idea of female empowerment and then putting women in the position where they can decide for themselves.

GJ: It is odd because the advice to women to not dress like sluts actually presupposes that women have a certain amount of agency. It is assuming that they have some power and that it is within their power to be less likely to be a target of rape. Yet feminists think that by giving women this advice would somehow trying to objectify them. I don't get it.

I guess the assumption that they really want to push across is that women are not agents, that they are entirely victims and entirely passive when it comes to the phenomenon of rape. There is nothing that they could do to avoid it. Instead of trying to spare them from rape I guess we are trying to just control them in some mean way. It is really a mentality of a spoilt child. Are these adults coming up with this nonsense?

HM: Right. We often get feminists argue that, "You shouldn't tell women not to dress like sluts; you should tell men not to rape." And it is kind of like saying you shouldn't tell kids to look both ways when they cross streets. You should tell cars not to hit them.

GJ: Yeah. That's good. And of course, society already tells men not to rape. And in fact, it punishes them quite severely when they are caught and convicted. I guess the assumption here is that we just haven't done enough to oppress and shame and tread upon men yet. We can't really criticize women. Nor even can we make recommendations for prudential measures to avoid being raped.

HM: Well, rape is one aspect of the anti slut-shaming argument. But it is even broader than that. More broadly, it is about saying women should be able to be sluts. They should be able to have promiscuous sex if they want to. The feminists would argue that society attempts to morally oppress and stigmatize that behavior, which is a form of oppression. And in doing that we are attempting to control them, and they are saying don't try to control us, don't tell us what to do, which is to me a logical argument. Whether or not I agree with it. The moving parts of the machine all add up. When you call a woman a slut, that is a form of punishment.

GJ: It's moral shaming. It's a negative term that is used to stigmatize certain forms of behavior so that it doesn't happen again. I think this is just another version of the whole double standard criticism then. If a man has many sexual partners, he is just a stud, and if a woman does, she is a slut, and that's a bad thing.

But you know, there are reasons for those double standards. One of them being promiscuity for women has worse consequences potentially than promiscuity for men. For a man, sperm is cheap. It doesn't cost men much to produce it and get it out of their system, whereas, eggs are expensive and rare. And if one of them happens to be impregnated, a woman is really stuck with it, barring abortion.

Given that attitudes about promiscuity go way back before the invention of birth-control pills and abortion, and, probably, to tell you the truth, back before the emergence of modern *Homo sapiens*, these are going to be deep-seated attitudes, biologically based double-standards between men and women. But let's not just make it a conversation about feminism. Let's get to the point you want to make about racism using this basic analysis.

HM: So, what I find interesting about this argument about slut-shaming is they are not saying "Don't call us sluts." What they are saying is that there is nothing wrong in being a slut. You shouldn't try to shame that behavior. You should accept that behavior. I think the most prominent attack on female promiscuity comes from a moral perspective. Traditionally, people would say it's immoral to be a slut and so sexually promiscuous. It seems to me what's happening is that if there is no underlying morality for a society then it is easy to make that argument. It is easy to say, "Hey, you are pushing this morality on me, but what it is based on? You are telling me it is immoral to be a slut, but where is that argument coming from?" At a slut walk, I saw one of the feminists holding up a sign that said "Slut is a social construct."

Applying the technology of this argument to racism, I think there is a parallel there in a sense that they (slut-shaming and racism) are both socially constructed ideas; to attack women for being sluts or to attack Europeans for being racists. The term that comes to my mind is "racism-shaming." If I say "Hey, I am a European, and I have a business to help my own people, and for that reason I am only going to employ Europeans, and I am not going to employ any other people," a Marxist would point at me and say "Hey, you are a racist. It is evil of you to do that. It is bad for you to put your own people first." So, it's the same structure of an argument as if you want to attack for being sexually promiscuous. The attempt is to oppress the assertion of our interests through stigmatization.

GJ: Right. So, is it your view then that when you called a racist we should act like a feminist-educated woman who is being called a slut and basically say, "Look, there is nothing wrong in being a racist, this is just a socially constructed word, and we don't accept the negative stigma that you want to attach to us with this word?" Is that your argument then?

HM: It's almost like that. Whereas the feminists say that "slut" is a social construct and pull the rug out from under the concept of the slut, I would like to apply the same argument to this term called "racism." I don't have any respect for the term "racism." It is a bullshit idea. It is not evil or immoral to stand up for our interests. On the contrary, it is our responsibility to do so. Because the problem with the term "racism" is that it is a loaded term like slut. A loaded term does more than simply describes objectively what is in front of you.

GJ: A non-loaded description of a slut would be a woman who is promiscuous sexually.

HM: Yes, that would be a less loaded way of saying it. Another example of a loaded term would the term "fag" as opposed to "homosexual," as the former comes loaded with negative connotations. You are implying something further than what is actually there, which is that there is something bad or evil or immoral about that behavior.

GJ: Right. Like "negro" or "black person" vs. "nigger."

HM: Yeah. What is a "nigger"? A "nigger" is a black person, but you are implying there is something evil or bad about being a black person. And the same thing with this idea of "racism." You call someone a racist you are implying inherent to the term "racism" is this suggestion of evil.

GJ: Right. Now with the term "racism," there is a whole complex of associations that comes to mind. For instance, when you talk about "racism" you think of people who get off on using racial epithets, telling racial jokes, putting down people of other races, perhaps, because they feel like to need to lord it over somebody. There is a whole aura of very negative things that goes along with that term. I don't like people who are constantly using racial epithets and putting other races down. I look down on them. I do admit that sometimes racist jokes are funny. I won't deny that they are funny, but I look down on that. There is something wrong with that.

But there is also something that is being identified with the term "racist" that's very good, namely, having a preference for your own kind. And again, that is a pre-human, biological imperative. We all think that a mother who neglects her own baby because she is more interested in the neighbor's baby for some reason has something wrong with her. There's something monstrous about that behavior. And, yet, on the international stage in relations between races, it's been defined as evil across the board for a white person to prefer another white person to a person of a different race just insofar as he is white. Why? Because they are more closely related to us. This is wired into the brain that people naturally feel more comfortable around people who are genetically similar to them. And they feel anxiety and discomfort among people who are genetically dissimilar. And these phenomena are part of our nature as animals. We can't get rid of it even if we thought it was a good thing. And it actually helps us perpetuate our own kind, stay safe, and so forth. These are all moral and good in my opinion.

So when people use the term "racist," one way that I handle it is to say, "Look, if by 'racist' you mean somebody who is using racial epithets, really gets off demeaning and degrading members of other races, that's not a good thing. I look down upon that myself, even if I might occasionally laugh at an A. Wyatt Mann cartoon or something like that. I still look down on that. I look down on myself for that. On the other hand, if you are taking about love of one's own, having genetic preferences for people who are genetically similar to you, there is nothing wrong with that."

I would just be inclined to say, "Look, I am not guilty of first bad form of racism. With minor exceptions, I laugh at jokes; let's be real. But I am totally 'guilty' of racism in the sense of having a love for one's own. But I don't feel bad about that. I think it's natural, normal, and right." And my inclination would be to say. "Well, I'll own up to that kind of racism. But if that is racism, then there is nothing wrong about the idea at all."

HM: Right. Part of the idea of this essay is how do you respond when people accuse you of racism. The two most common responses are that "Hey, we are not the racists; they are the real racists." I try to deflect the attack. Or "Yes, I am a racist. What's wrong with that?" And that is kind of similar to the slut argument.

GJ: "Yeah, I'm a racist. So what?"

HM: Yeah. These are the two most common responses. I argue that we shouldn't do either of those. If you think of the attack as the sword that is coming at you, you shouldn't fall on the sword by saying, "Yes, I am a racist." Nor should you deflect it. You should shatter the sword, by which I mean deconstructing the concept of "racism." Are you accusing me of standing up for my own people? Of course, I am doing that, but to call it racism is problematic because inherent to the term is the suggestion of immorality.

GJ: Right. Well, in a way, you are saying it's not a bad thing. If I were to refer to a black person as a "nigger," that would be immediately interpreted as "Oh, there is that racist being mean." But I hear black people call one another "nigger" all the time. What are they doing there? They know that when a white person or a non-black person says the word "nigger," they are putting them down. And one of the ways they defuse its negativity is by owning it. They are saying that "Yeah, I am a nigger, but there is nothing wrong with being a nigger." Like "I am a slut, but there is nothing wrong with being a slut." Or "I am a racist, but there is nothing wrong with that."

In a way, I think that is shattering the sword. It's not falling on it, because the real sting of it is the negative moral connotation that society attaches to it. And when they throw the racism bomb at you, you grab it and defuse it. How do you defuse it? You basically deny the negativity that they want to associate with it. They make that hard, because it's all loaded up. All these negative pictures of Klansmen burning crosses and lynching negroes and people being assholes and telling racist jokes and all that kind of stuff. They are masters of packing in a whole bunch of negative pictures and stories connected with racism. That is part of the propaganda.

And my feeling as to how to get rid of it is just to say it is not simply bad a thing; you are trying to cast negative aspersions on something that is natural, normal, and right. In fact, it is something that, if you are honest, you will yourself admit to doing, because most people feel comfortable around their own kind. Most liberals who are massively anti-racist will still have a preference for their own children over the children of strangers.

Occasionally, you get these people like Mia Farrow who have one of every color. But, honestly, I think Angelina Jolie would probably admit feeling closer to the natural children of her own body than the adopted children she has from Africa and southeast Asia.

So, I think if we try to make it real and bring it down to the fact that we feel more comfortable around people who are like us, like our families and our children, than the people outside that, the argument could be stretched to our race, i.e., our extended family. And there is nothing bad about that. And as long as everybody gets to do the same thing, like blacks take care of blacks and Asians take care of Asians and whites take care of whites, we are all going to be alright. It strikes me that that approach is good.

One thing that I have done in discussing these issues with a friend, who is honest, but she is not predisposed to the things I stand for, like White Nationalism, is to begin with twins. She has met identical twins, and she sees how identical twins are really close, to the point they can complete one another's sentences and read one another's thoughts. We know that identical twins raised apart make astonishingly similar decisions on things that are so trivial you wouldn't think they are genetically determined. They vote the same political party. They drive the same make and color car. They date women with similar hair colors. They have similar professions and so forth. All of these things are genetic. Psychologically, the intimacy that twins have is remarkable. Years ago, I met a pair of twins, and one said—and I am sure the other agreed—that they were not so much two people as "one egg divided." I thought that was really beautiful. I think we can extend that sense of community and closeness on the analogy of twins. The closer people are to us genetically, the more natural harmony we feel with them. We understand them intuitively. We are more likely to able to cooperate with them.

Let's say there is a problem in your neighborhood. You want to put speed bumps on the road. Or you want to clean up the creek that runs through your neighborhood. It is going to be easier if people live around you are like you. If they trust the same way you trust, they feel responsibility in the same way that you feel responsibility. But those things are racially and culturally quite variable. If you live in a racially and culturally mixed neighborhood, it is very difficult to get the neighbors to come together to get things like speed bumps or keep the streets clean or enforce any kind of standards. I am trying to bring it down to things like that, and I think if you do that, people realize that there is a natural preference, which is not such a bad thing.

But then why is racism the number one crime? And let's face it, the only thing sacred these days is anti-racism for a lot of people. Certainly, within the churches that is the only thing that is sacred. I think if we can break it down and get people to think about their own actual decisions and not just confront them with the fact that when they have kids they move to "safer areas" with "better schools," I think we can get people to get a bit more real about that and take away that negative sting that the term has been loaded with by anti-white propaganda.

HM: Right. I am a nationalist, and I agree that it is totally legitimate for us to stand up for our interests, but I will never call myself a racist. Inherently, it is an attack. If anyone ever called me a racist, I'd just say my approach is that there is nothing wrong with standing up for our interests, but at the same time I would imitate the African-American argument of "Don't call us niggers." I would say "Don't call me a racist. It offends me that you call me a racist, because you are saying it is evil for my ethnic group to assert our interests."

GJ: Right. So, we come back to the same thing, which is basically that we have to unburden ourselves of the claim that this is evil. We either reject evil along with the term itself, or we say "Look, the term is fine, but it's not evil." We don't have to choose between one and the other. It might be useful to use both approaches, just in different circumstances and contexts. I can feign indignation if people call me a racist, but I would definitely explain there isn't anything wrong in taking care of my own.

One thing, Hugh, that we do need to keep in mind is that people are strongly motivated by morality. The real issue is what's right and wrong. But there is another element to human psychology, and that is that sometimes bad things are very attractive. Specifically, people who are willing to own up to being a bit of a scoundrel, who aren't afraid and don't show fear of having a finger pointed at them, there is something lordly about that.

HM: I agree.

GJ: Women like bad boys with a little hint of bad about them. Men find bad girls useful, but they don't particularly admire them. Anyway, it is not always good to be good, but at times it is good to be a little bad. And I think in this particular case we do not want to say we are bad, but what we really do need to communicate that we are not afraid to be *called* bad. We are willing to hazard that. We are willing to stand up to that. And we are not willing to accept it in the privacy of our own thoughts. They can call us bad. They can heap abuse upon us. We are not going to accept the negative connotation. Sometimes you just say, "Sure, whatever. You can call whatever you want. It is not going to deflect me from doing the right thing, and that is taking care of my own."

HM: Absolutely, I agree with this idea. I often say rebellion is the essence of cool.

GJ: Oh, totally. What does cool mean? Well, in the low sense it just means what fashion is being promoted at the time and what crap is being sold to you. What is cool about James Dean? What is cool about Clint Eastwood's classic cowboy roles? I think he is the quintessence of cool. It is a kind of lordly, aloof quality. It connotes strength, right?

HM: I would never deny that, absolutely, I am putting my people first. I prefer the term European nationalist but really, I mean White Nationalist. It is one and the same thing. My only hesitation in using the term European nationalist is because sometimes people misunderstand me and think that I am talking about some kind of European civic nationalism and my loyalty to people who are citizens of the legal entity called Europe. You know, countries within the continent of Europe. But obviously I am referring to white people. And that in itself is a subversive, dangerous, and rebellious thing to say.

But still, I would never call myself a racist, because it is offensive to me. It is like it is bad of us to stand up for our interests. And it is just like how African Americans say they would never tolerate us calling them "niggers." And in the same way the term racism is an epithet the same way "nigger" is. And it is an epithet applicable primarily to people of our ethnic group. You hear this argument more frequently from the Marxists who say that white people can't experience racism and that white supremacy and racism go hand in hand. The European white is inherent to the concept of racism. To be a racist and to be a white person is one and the same thing. Only white people can be racists, because we have been beneficiaries of a white supremacist system.

GJ: Right.

HM: So, it even offends me to hear fellow nationalist Europeans who are white using the term "racist," because the mere usage implies the illegitimacy of our cultural and political existence. It is a kind of acknowledgement that it is bad of us to assert ourselves.

GJ: I see what you are saying, but I don't agree. In a way I don't want to argue with the word so much as I want to argue over what's really dangerous about the word, which is that stigmatizing tone that is attached to it. The stigma is the problem, not the word. And if we can separate the word and the stigma, it is fine.

But here's the thing: I don't want them to make us dance. Think of the cowboy movies. They are firing at your feet and making you dance. Somebody shoots at my feet, I am going to move my feet. But if somebody says the word "racist" to me, I'd say "Are you kidding? Grow up. Come on." I am not going to dance to that tune or get excited about it. And my feeling is that the coolest and most subversive thing is to just say "Look, you call me whatever you want. It is not going to deflect me from doing the right thing, which is taking care of my own." That's how I feel about it.

It weakens us if we hold the idea that the term "racist" *ipso facto* is stigmatizing, and it offends us to be called racists. Of course it offends me that there are people who want my kind to cease to exist. I would like to pluck that idea out of the world. I would like that to be gone. The words they use are neither here nor there. It is the evil intent that I am really worried about. And

I don't want to be caught up in word games. Especially, I don't want to leave the power in the word.

In a way, my criticism of what you are saying is that it leaves the power in the word. You say it offends you inherently. The word inherently stigmatizes. But my view is that nothing inherently stigmatizes, and nothing should inherently offend except the evil intention behind the use of this word. I want to fight that evil, and if the word doesn't scare me, and we can teach our people not to get scared by the word, then it loses its power, and people who say that just sound like idiots.

I think we would be turning a corner towards victory when somebody says "That's racist" and people just laugh out loud. They don't even feel the need to defend themselves or the need to say "Yeah, whatever." They just laugh. When we get to the point when people just laugh at that, I think we are there.

So, I don't want to give them as much as you are giving them, because if you think the term is inherently against us, then we are going to be ducking and weaving, and I don't want to do that. I don't want these people to make me dance with a simple word. We just need to laugh these things off and go about our business. "O racism, where is thy sting?" That's the attitude I want our people to have.

I think what you are saying is a stage along the way to getting there. I would like us to be impervious to the charge. When we see these politicians and media people who make some unguarded statements, and then they are being roasted, and they are just blubbering for forgiveness for their horrible crime of noticing something real, I pity these people. I want to take their hand, and sit them down, and say "It's just a word that is being used by evil people who are out to destroy you."

These people might pretend they are offering you a path to absolution. That's just to sway people to working against racism if they think they can absolve themselves of this guilt. But there is just no absolution, because what we are trying to absolve ourselves of is natural, normal, and right. It is hardwired into our nature as healthy organisms. The only way to overcome this is to become a sick, twisted, and mangled organism. And the harder people try to become "anti-racist," the more twisted and sicker they become as people.

HM: This idea of power and putting us on the defensive and if we respond negatively to the accusation of racism, we are putting the power in their hands.

GJ: Yeah. They are putting us on trial.

HM: I think actually getting upset about the term puts us in the power seat. It actually puts them on the defensive if you can say, "Don't call me a 'racist'"; it is an empowering thing. Like for a black to say, "Don't call me 'nigger,'" especially when he says, "It is okay for me to say it, but it is not okay for you to say it." It puts them in a position where they can talk down to us. It puts us on the defensive. It puts us in a position where we say, "Oh sorry, it's not okay for us to say it." And by them getting upset about it, it gives them an opportunity to attack. It is the same way native Americans getting upset about the term "The Washington Redskins."

GJ: Right.

HM: Why are they getting upset about the term? My perspective is by getting upset it gives them an opportunity to attack. It puts them on the offensive and us on the defensive. I think most native Americans don't actually get offended by the term, but this gives them on an ego level an opportunity to attack. It creates a power hierarchy that puts them at the top. My approach is the same to this term "racism." "Don't call me a racist."

I don't call black people "niggers." Even in private I don't call them "niggers." That, honestly, is a literal truth. I am already a White Nationalist, and I would not want to make more enemies for petty things like using terms like that. I don't call black people "niggers." I don't call Jews "kikes." I don't call Asians "chinks." And the reason I don't call them that, especially to their faces, is simply out of respect. Like I don't call people names because I don't want to offend them. My attitude is "Hey, if you expect us no to call you names, then we expect to be shown the same respect in return. We don't call you names, don't call us names." You calling me a racist means it's bad that I stand for my interests. You are trying to oppress that behavior through stigmatization. It is like saying it is evil of us to do what is good for us. That's my thinking.

GJ: Right. I remember one time this guy was going off on me on the internet about something, and I responded, "You're the one on trial here, not me." And the truth of the matter was that I put him on trial simply by saying that. I simply switched the dynamics by asserting I am not on trial, but you are. And any time we can do that is positive. You put them on the defensive as you are recommending, by saying that calling a white person racist is the equivalent of calling a black person a "nigger."

Or you could just attack by saying "Why do you hate white people?" I would not say "Do you hate white people?" because then it's a "No." Technically, the former is a loaded question. And if they deny that they hate white people, then we say "Why do you stigmatize what's normal for every other race, which is taking care of our own?"

The point is we need to stop being on the defensive and start going on the offensive. Whenever these people start lobbing the racism word at us, we need to go on the offense. The *way* we do it is less an issue than just *doing it*. We have to do it. We have to stop being on the defensive about this, because there is nothing wrong with it. Maybe the word is not the word we want to use, but the substance that they are trying to stigmatize is definitely something we have to defend. We have to totally reject the idea that we are guilty.

This is one of the things that really bothers me about a lot of White Nationalists. They think White Nationalism is some kind of a dirty joke. They think of it as something a little illicit, a little off-color, not for mixed or polite company. They look around and act like they are about to tell a dirty joke before they launch into this stuff. It communicates entirely the wrong attitude.

I think we need to be unapologetic, self-assured, self-righteous about this stuff without sounding brittle and hysterical. An American-Jewish journalist named Max Blumenthal went to Israel and filmed Israeli Jews running down Obama. Oh, the scandal, the scandal. Everyone was supposed to be upset. One Jewish fellow quite impressed me. It was less what he said than how he said it. He said, "They don't understand. This land is ours." He said it in a totally unapologetic manner. It wasn't strident. It wasn't hysterical. It was just a firm, matter-of-fact declaration that this land was theirs, and they were going to defend it. And I know if white people or nationalists could be that cool and matter-of-fact and non-apologetic and non-off-color about asserting our interests, we'd be a lot further down the road.

So, I think we agree on the basic goal.

HM: I think I have to make the argument a little sharper, because you are still not convinced. [laughs]

GJ: Yeah. I am still not convinced, but you know . . . you have made some progress here, I have to admit.

HM: I think I did especially the way you used the word "stigmatize." It's important for us to use that word. In calling white people "racist," it is an attempt to oppress, stigmatize, and marginalize the assertion of our interests.

GJ: Exactly. That's well put.

HM: The whole point of the essay is to appreciate that this is an attempt to control us the same way. In psychological terms, it's called "conditioning." You want an organism to do something, you give it a positive reinforcement, and if you don't want a behavior, you give it something bad. The term "racism" is an attack. It is a punishment. It is a form of conditioning. They are trying to hurt you for things they don't approve of. They say, "Good white people don't stand up for their interests. Good white people shut up and sit down. Good white people don't do what's good for them. Good white people do what's good for me." And they reward you for being a good, obedient Leftist, and they punish you for standing up for your interests.

GJ: I think it's important for people who are being attacked to stand up against it. But I think it's important for other people to stand up for them when they are being attacked. I think a lot of our motivation boils down to the fact that we take stock of what our fellows are going to do in a situation. And we know that if we going to be out there alone, and no one is going to come to our defense, we are not going to take any risks. Why do it alone? That is what most people think. It takes a very special and rare kind of person to stand up and to do things when they can be pretty much assured that nobody will come to their defense.

If more and more instances take place in which people come to the defense of somebody who is under attack, then it is going to encourage people. This is why I think the attacks are so brutal. They are so brutal against somebody who offends the racial dogmas today, because the people in power know that if somebody states the truth—un-PC truth—and is not slapped down and made to apologize or made an example of, then other people will be emboldened.

One project that I have talked over, which actually never got off the drawing board because we don't know the right people to do it, is to put together a crack team of people who could do the following. First we sit down and we do an analysis of the process by which a person who has offended the dominant diversity cult is brought under pressure to apologize, his job is taken away, whatever. We need to find out the steps of that process, and then we need to figure out ways the process can be interrupted at each stage.

So the next time some story like Paula Deen breaks, we send in really sharp-looking, well-spoken people with credentials, like lawyers, sit them down, and lay out what's going on. We show them examples of people who have been destroyed, even though they apologized, and we try to convince them that first of all they should stand their ground. I call it the "Stand Your Ground Project." We would give people what they need to stand their ground. We give them legal advice. We would say that we can mobilize a certain amount of public opinion. We'll get the BUGS people swarming internet chatrooms and comment threads. If we can give people the resources, moral support, and technical advice that they need to stand their ground and not apologize, and if a few people do that, it is going to catch on.

I think most white people in America and Canada don't believe this diversity stuff anymore. And they are being suppressed because they think that they are alone, and if somebody who is mildly famous speaks up and they see them pilloried in public, they go back to thinking they're alone and helpless. I think that if a few people who are somewhat public stand their ground and don't back down and are not destroyed, that could really be game changing.

So, part of the discussion we are having today really fits into to teaching people how to resist, to stand up against that kind of charge. But we need to do more than just give them talking points and moral certainty. We also need to figure out how to give them the support they need for standing their ground. We need to help people actually negotiating a real crisis. And if more people do that, I think things will change.

HM: Yeah.

GJ: So, are there any final thoughts on this?

HM: I think it's good to wrap up now, and then I'd like to have a discussion with you another time maybe. I want to talk about morality as a whole other thing.

GJ: Oh yeah, definitely.

HM: For now, I think I have used up all my ammunition trying to make an argument about this term "racism."

GJ: Well, it has really been thought-provoking for me, and those who are listening in are going to be thinking hard too. I'd like to do more conversations like this. Not just an interview but a conversation. I think it's valuable.

HM: Yeah. Good. Okay, thank you.

GJ: Well, thank you, Hugh.

Counter-Currents, September 16, 2019

Answering Sargon of Akkad:

An Interview with Millennial Woes*

Millennial Woes: Hello, this is Millennial Woes, and I'm going to ask Greg Johnson the questions from Sargon of Akkad's questionnaire for the Alt Right. There are eight questions, and I'll ask each one, and then Greg can give his answer.

Do you want to talk about Sargon and the skeptic community before we begin? It's probably not relevant. I think everyone knows that already.

Greg Johnson: Everyone probably knows that, and I know nothing about Sargon, really, and the skeptic community, so I don't have anything to say. I just had an introduction to it today when a person sent an article to *Counter-Currents* about the skeptic war on YouTube with the Alt Right, and I thought, "Well, this is interesting," so that's when I looked and found the eight questions that Sargon has posed to the Alt Right—or, as I want to put it, White Nationalists—so I thought I should answer these or give it a try. But then I thought my life is too short, and sitting down and grinding this out in written form is too laborious. I have other important things I need to do. And you suggested we just have a conversation about it, so I think that's a great way forward.

MW: Exactly. It's nice, it's off the cuff, it won't take too much time, and then we can move on to other things. This is why I want to do more livestreaming this year, so there's less worrying about it all.

Okay, here we go with the first question. "Are Jews oppressing white people?" And I'm not sure if I should say anything. I

---

* The following is a transcript of a conversation between Greg Johnson and Millennial Woes recorded in January of 2018. I would like to thank SC for the transcript.

think it's obvious that these questions come from a certain perspective and are designed to elicit certain answers in order to produce a certain impression of White Nationalism.

GJ: Right. He's obviously grandstanding to his audience, and, just judging from the questions, he is presupposing that his audience holds certain principles or values that I find questionable and that White Nationalists generally reject. So he's in effect framing this in a way that's appealing to the prejudices of his audience, and instead of raising those underlying value questions, he's just presupposing those questions.

So in answering them, I want to do two things. First of all, I'll answer the question in a straightforward way, but I also want to identify the false underlying premise that he smuggles in and that he's depending upon in the minds of his audience.

MW: Right. Excellent. Well, okay. Here's the first question. "Are Jews oppressing white people?"

GJ: Yes. Jews are oppressing white people. White Nationalists like me and Kevin MacDonald argue that the current political, economic, and cultural system in the West is basically inimical to the interests of the founding white populations of every Western country. This anti-white system—which features such things as multiculturalism, denigration of whites, denigration of white heritage, erasure of white heritage, creating movies where historically white characters are being played by nonwhites, open borders, race replacement immigration, promotion of miscegnation for whites, and so on—has been constructed by the Jewish intellectual and cultural elite, precisely to harm the interests of the majority white populations of every European country.

They have been so successful in shaping people's perceptions, values, and narratives that most white people are now marching self-righteously into the graveyard. They're self-righteously pursuing policies that will destroy our race in the long-term. They're exalting white guilt and white self-abasement. They're amplifying and encouraging the ethnocentrism and grievances of nonwhites. They're welcoming refugees.

They're adopting black babies, and they're signaling about this on social media, and so forth. These people have been brainwashed, essentially, by the elites. They've been brainwashed with a message that's constructed by Jewish intellectual movements who are calculatedly creating a political system and a culture that are inimical to white interests.

The very whites who actually speak out against this — who see through the brainwashing, who see that these trends are inimical to the interests of our people and if they're not interrupted, are going to lead to the extinction of the white race — are actively oppressed by the Jewish community.

When the Greek government goes to New York City and speaks to powerful international Jews, and are ordered to arrest the leaders of the Golden Dawn party in Greece, and they go home and arrest the Golden Dawn leadership, that is active, open, naked, Jewish oppression of self-conscious white people.

When Jewish organizations like the SPLC and the ADL create lists of individuals and organizations and websites that need to be de-platformed, and these are de-platformed, that is active, open Jewish oppression.

So my answer is yes, Jews are oppressing white people. They are oppressing white people to the full extent that they need to oppress white people to attain their long-term goals, which is basically driving whites to extinction.

MW: Would you say that a better word here would be "subverting" than "oppressing"? Because "oppression" implies a sort of heavy-handed, open, overt authority clamping down openly, and publicly, and unashamedly on a populace, whereas I think what's going on here is more akin to subversion from behind the scenes.

GJ: Yes, well, they have subverted us to the extent that's possible, and for the whites that can't be brainwashed and bought and intimidated into going along with their agenda, then there's open oppression. National Action has been declared a terrorist group in England, and its members are being arrested. That is oppression in the colorful sense that he's trying to paint when he uses that word, "oppression."

Now as to the underlying assumptions in the minds of his audience, the prejudices in the minds of his audience that Sargon is appealing to here: they are complex, but a couple things come to mind. First of all, he's pandering to colorful pictures of totalitarian oppression, jack-booted thugs, and so forth. They do send jack-booted thugs out, but that's not the primary way that they rule us. They rule us through soft power, through metapolitics, through brainwashing, intimidation, corruption, and subversion.

But when those fail, then they will, of course, go to hard power. They will arrest the leaders of political parties; they will de-platform websites; they will arrest members of organizations.

They do that too, but they don't have to do that for the most part, and the people who think they aren't being oppressed by Jews are basically the ones who are brainwashed into going along with their own oppression, who censor their own thoughts so they don't need to be censored.

The other thing I think that he's trying to appeal to is the classic horseshoe theory. "The SJWs claim that they're being oppressed, and you claim that you're being oppressed, so you're just the SJWs of the Right!," something *jejune*, something childish like that.

Another thing he might be appealing to is a primitive, manospherian psychology that basically holds that we should never admit that we're being oppressed because that sounds weak. You don't want to admit that you're weak. You don't want to admit that you're oppressed.

Try that argument on the blacks who led the Civil Rights movement. Try that argument on any anti-colonial movement. "You don't want to seem weak by admitting that you're oppressed." That really is an argument that the oppressor would want to circulate. "You don't want to admit that this vast Indian subcontinent is so weak and disorganized that it could be ruled by a relative handful of foreigners, do you? Wouldn't you be humiliated to admit that?"

Of course it is humiliating. It is humiliating to be oppressed by a small, vicious group of people, and we need to deal with the full weight of that humiliation, the full horror of that reality.

Then we need to get mad. Then we need to get busy doing something about it.

So those are some of the false assumptions trailing along in the nimbus of this particular question.

MW: Question two: "Should interracial couples be forced to separate?"

GJ: I guess we're supposed to think of poor Romeo and Juliet and their horrible families trying to pull them apart. My answer to this question is: No. I wouldn't force interracial couples to separate. I would force them to leave the country if I were creating an ethnically homogeneous white society. I would say: "You married a Japanese woman. Why don't you go to Japan?" I wouldn't force couples to separate.

The important thing is not forcing couples to separate. The important thing is to lay down laws that would prevent them from getting together in the first place. That's what an ethnostate needs to have, and many countries, including the United States, through long stretches of its history, have had laws that prevent people from marrying outside of their race. That is something that has existed throughout most of history, whenever different races live in proximity. Laws on the books, or customs that enforce the same results. Frankly, we need to go back to that. We need to go back to a situation where we value the purity and integrity of our race, the distinctness of our race, and therefore we do not permit interracial marriages to happen in the first place.

And the couples that exist today, well, if we're going to be partitioning countries and creating homogeneous ethnostates, they can leave. But I wouldn't force anyone to get a divorce. No. I would just simply say, "You should go to Hong Kong or Singapore or Africa or wherever you found your bride." New Africa, whatever. We'll deal with it that way.

As for Romeo and Juliet, the parents were right. It was a terrible idea for these silly, starry-eyed kids to try to marry when they came from families that had been at war with one another and had killed members of one another for a very long time. There's simply no possible happy ending for something like that. So I think it is rather silly that we can cite that tragedy as somehow a premise to forestall any sensible policies to arrest the alarming trend towards miscegnation in white societies.

MW: Okay, and what are the underlying presumptions that Sargon is playing on here?

GJ: I think he is just playing on the romantic idea that if people love one another it would be a terrible tragedy to break them apart. Also, I guess he's trying to paint pictures of jack-booted thugs tearing people apart. Honestly, he can try to do that, but the proper view to take when you're making policy is not to think about the picturesque and tear-jerking incidents that enforcing any law can lead to.

Rather, we must think about the invisible couples in the future that race-mixing is preventing from coming together, and the invisible white generations that you're making possible by protecting the race from being bred out of existence through miscegnation. That's what we need to focus on when making policy. We need to focus on the invisible people that we're saving, rather than a few picturesque things that can be staged and put in the media, like these pictures of Mexicans posing by border fences blubbering and touching one another through the wire. If they're so sad to be separate, why don't they just all go back to Mexico and be together? So, he's just engaged in some kind of low emotional blackmail.

But we should definitely prevent interracial couples from getting together in the first place. That should be policy. Return to anti-miscegnation laws. But the best form of miscegnation laws are the basically the *de facto* anti-miscegnation laws of having one's own country. If the races are separate from one another, and you just don't go to school with, or on dates with, or to college with people of different races, you're not going to fall in love with them.

MW: Question three. "Should the government prevent citizens from leaving the country in order to preserve the race?"

GJ: I guess he's trying to conjure up an image of the Berlin wall. I love that. Years ago, Rush Limbaugh, when he was being a real sophist and open borders advocate, would always try to characterize building a wall on the border as the Berlin Wall, which kept people in, as opposed to building a wall to keep invaders out. I guess that's what Sargon's trying to say. We wouldn't allow breeding stock to leave the country. I think that's kind of silly.

My view of how to create an ethnostate is basically to draw boundaries and create incentives for people to sort themselves out. That means that if I were dictator of America tomorrow, I would encourage all the people who can't get behind that idea, even if they're lily-white and as blonde and blue-eyed as you can possibly imagine, to leave. The way to get what we want is to give people the option of living in a society that's homogeneous—and to give the ones who don't agree with that the option of leaving.

That will create a population with a broad consensus that it's okay to be white and to want to live among white people. You won't want people who undermine that social consensus, so why force them to stay? I like the idea of allowing people to voluntarily sort themselves out into different communities. You can "ethnically cleanse" and ideologically cleanse the ethnostate by just allowing the people who don't believe in it to go live in a multicultural society if they want.

I wrote an article at *Counter-Currents* called "The Slow Cleanse" about how we could have an orderly, humane process of "ethnic cleansing" that would go on for, say, fifty years. Basically we'd create incentives for nonwhites within a particular territory to move. We would encourage the younger ones, the ones who have kids, to move. The older ones, we wouldn't care about, because they'll just grow old and die.

People move all the time. They move all the time for jobs, they move all the time for college, and so forth, and we would just have a policy where, say, if an Asian family works for a multi-national corporation that moves them around occasionally, the next move they would go outside the United States, or outside the ethnostate somewhere else.

If you simply had policies in place like that for fifty years, we would get to an ethnostate, and it wouldn't involve any sort of jack-booted thugs and totalitarian stuff, trains full of plaintive looking people being shipped off, that we've been trained to envision by a hundred Holocaust movies, or a thousand Holocaust movies, however many there have been.

So I think that we should definitely allow people to leave the country if they want to, and that would be a way of preserving the race. Even though they might be good white people, if they're not behind the idea that it's okay to be white, and for whites to live amongst their own kind and prefer their own kind, we prefer that they would go somewhere else.

MW: Okay, question four. "Should the state control education?"

GJ: Certainly. Of course, I think the state needs to control education. One of the primary functions of the state is to cultivate the populace. The reason we need state-controlled education is to create unity and to instill virtue, as well as to give people the information they need to survive and to prosper. The purpose of government is to lay the foundations for living a good life in society, and the right kind of education is essential to that.

Again, there's information, there are skills, and there are also virtues. Virtue should be one of the things that we strive to instill through education, and if we have state controlled education, and we create a sufficiently virtuous populace — a populace in which people can control their behavior, think ahead, govern themselves, and act ethically in their dealings with others — then when they grow up, you have a society that's almost self-regulating, and so you don't need cops rushing to intervene all the time in, say, the domestic abuse problems of a particular couple. There's going to be less of that. There will be fewer people treating each other in unethical ways, committing crimes, etc., if we raise a virtuous populace that has basically the same values and feel like they're part of a society, feel responsible to the society, etc. So yes, definitely the state should control education.

Now of course, Sargon is trying to paint a picture of propaganda and brainwashing. The Left definitely needs to control education because the things they value and promote are false, and if you allow people to think for themselves, or have a quiet moment of reflection away from the telescreen blaring propaganda, they're going to start thinking for themselves, and the power of the Left is going to unravel.

But we don't have to worry about that so much because what we teach is in harmony with nature.

However, just because it's in harmony with nature doesn't mean that we can just let everybody sort it out for themselves, because there are better or worse ways of doing things, and the better way is to have an orderly society where people are cultivated from very early age to have common language and customs, to have the necessary information and skills to do well in life, and to have the virtues to behave nobly and to be self-actualized. Those are things that the state needs to get involved in, and those are things that go with the grain of nature, rather than against it, and will produce a society in which people flourish and are happy.

MW: But I think the objection that could be raised to this is "What if you're a parent and you don't like the education that the state is giving your child?" I mean, should home-schooling be available? Should private schooling be available?

GJ: These make sense in societies that are already in a bad state. Either societies that are rotted from the start with radical individualism, low trust, "devil take the hindmost" attitudes towards different classes of people, a factionalized society—or a society where the people in charge of education and the state have interests inimical to the society as a whole, and therefore they're viewed with distrust as exploiters and propagandizers and so forth. So for those concerns to make sense, that is already presupposing a bad situation. A lot of people who believe in home-schooling, let's face it, are religious cranks, young Earth creationists who don't want their children to be exposed to the facts about evolution, and so forth. But if we were living in a really healthy society, I don't think there would be a movement for home-schooling. People would think they're part of a greater community and not want to keep their children home to educate them.

MW: But also, a lot of people who are White Nationalists believe in home-schooling because it's the only way they can get their child away from the cultural Marxist programming.

GJ: Why not home-schooling today and state schooling tomorrow? We should be totally pragmatic about these things. Home-schooling today means "Unplug your kids from the brainwashing machine." That's an important thing. But as a long-term solution, as soon as we have control, we're going to want to teach kids the proper message, therefore, compulsory public education should be a feature of an ethnostate, especially if we've got so much garbage to purge from our culture, so many false attitudes, so many false ideas, so many false values.

I am constantly surprising myself by stumbling across pieces of liberal propaganda in my own beliefs. I should know better. I have this term I call the "complete lifetime audit," the "total life audit." Once you get red-pilled, you really have to go through and audit everything that you've accepted over the course of your life, and you're going to find a lot of fossilized bits of propaganda that you haven't questioned, just stuck in your brain.

So if we create an ethnostate, we definitely need control of education. We'll have to spend a lot of time battling the remnants of false ideas in our society, to set things on the right course. I'm all for private education, home-schooling, and whatever today. But in the ethnostate we should definitely have state education.

MW: But should we have *just* state education?

GJ: Yes, we should just have state education, because we would want to make sure that everyone is on the same page and gets the same message.

MW: I disagree with you here, because for various reasons I just don't like the idea of a population being systematically programmed like that, but also what if the Left subverted the department of education in the ethnostate?

GJ: There would be no Left in the ethnostate. Not the Left that we have today. They would be some of the people that we wouldn't prevent from leaving the country. There would be political pluralism in the ethnostate, but there would not be a Left in the sense of the anti-white Left that we have today.

Basically, my view of how an ethnostate should work is this. We should have the maximum amount of pluralism and freedom as long as the degradation and destruction of the white race is not one of the political possibilities. We can vote on all kinds of stuff. We can quarrel about women's rights, and feminism, and abortion, and tax policies, and all of that kind of stuff.

But there should be no debate about whether it's good to be white, that whites have a right to continue to exist, etc. Those sorts of things should be off the table. There are sacred cows in our society today, and unfortunately those sacred cows are not in the interests of white people. So my attitude is we need maximum pluralism consistent with the preservation and flourishing of the white race. I call that notion "hegemony," the hegemony of pro-white ideas.

I have an essay in my book *New Right vs. Old Right* called "Hegemony." It's also at the *Counter-Currents* site, where I talk about hegemony as a form of soft power, and that's what we're ruled by today. Jews don't openly oppress most of us, because they enjoy hegemony over 99% of the minds of our people, and therefore it's only 1% of people who get uppity like us that they actually need actively oppress.

I think we need to replace Jewish hegemony, anti-white hegemony, anti-white soft power, with pro-white soft power, pro-white hegemony, and then we can go about our business, we can start businesses, we can take trips, we can have political parties, we can have political debates, we can quarrel with one another. But the destruction of our race is not something that will ever be allowed to be conceived as a possible political goal. That has to be taken off the table completely.

MW: Question five, and it's a similar sort of moral, ethical quandary. "Should the state control the media?"

GJ: Yes, the state should control the media. The question is *how* should the state control the media.

Let's revisit the education question, because you moved to the media question before I said one final thing about the educational question. If there is a solid hegemony of pro-white ideas, then that would allow for private education, because no matter whether you go to private school, or public school, or you do it at home, they're all going to be on the same page about the essential things, namely the preservation and flourishing of our race. So the kind of control of education that I really envision is going to be this soft power hegemony. Even homeschoolers are compelled to educate their children. It is not possible in the United States to simply say, "We're not going to educate our children at all." That is against the law, so the state is controlling homeschooling as well.

The issue is this: Does the state have to *provide* education, or does the state simply have to control the *central content* of education and make education *compulsory*? I would say the state doesn't necessarily have to provide education. Although that's a pretty good thing, frankly, and I would prefer that. But the state definitely will *control* it on the most essential issues, even if it's provided at home or at private academies.

The same principle applies with the media. In the modern situation today, there is a hegemony of anti-white, pro-multicultural ideas in the media. It doesn't matter if it's CNN or Fox. There are certain issues that are sacrosanct. They are anti-racist, and they will fight to the death against being called a racist, and that is the kind of hegemony that I think that we need to have over the media as well.

The state doesn't need to have active censors or run all the newspapers, or anything like that, if there is a sufficiently strong consensus on the essential issue of white survival. So the answer is hegemony, which is a form of control over the media, but it doesn't necessarily mean that all the media has to be owned by the state and all the content has to be provided by the state. But the essential parameters definitely need to be controlled.

There should be certain ideas that simply never get a serious hearing in a white ethnostate. Multiculturalism will never get a serious hearing in the white ethnostate. Liberalism will never get a serious hearing in the ethnostate. Marxism will never get a serious hearing. We will trot them out and talk about them as examples of the bad old days, but they are never going to get a serious hearing again. No one's ever going to try these terrible, destructive ideas again, and we would be fools and cucks just to set up a system with a suicide pact built into it. No serious society includes a suicide clause in its constitution. That's just absurd. Even liberal societies don't do that.

MW: Alright. Question six: "Should the state control the economy?"

GJ: Yes, the state should control the economy. But, again, *how* should the state control the economy? I guess Sargon is putting it in these terms like "state control of education," "state control of the media" to bring to mind the Soviet Union or some kind of fossilized Communist one-party system where everything is controlled by drab bureaucrats. It's *Nineteen Eighty-Four*.

But the state doesn't have to own every factory to control the economy. It simply has to exercise an *oversight function* to make sure that economic activity is consistent with the long-term health and welfare of the people. Therefore, no more globalization, free trade, open borders, all of those things that we're told are "good for the economy." They're good for *some* people's economies. Some interest groups. But not society as a whole. Those things need to be shut down. We will not have trade and economic policies that are bad for our race. We won't permit that.

Does that mean that every little aspect of the economy needs to be controlled? No, only essential aspects of the economy need to be controlled. Anything else should be a free-for-all. There should be as much freedom is as consistent with the common good. That's my answer to liberals.

Liberalism is a modern political philosophy that proclaims that the common good doesn't exist, or it can't be known, or if we can know it, it doesn't matter, or if we can know it, we can't pursue it, and therefore, basically, we just have to set up mechanisms whereby people can pursue private interests and somehow we have to hope that it all works out. I say phooey to that.

There is a common good. There are public goods. There is a meaningful sense of collectivism that every sensible society actually embodies, even ones that are quite individualistic in their day-to-day order, and we should have a modicum of collectivism so that when individual choices conflict with the common good, then the state steps in and says no. Where individual choices are conducive to the common good, or are neutral towards the common good, there's no need for the state to be involved at all.

My view is that it's probably not necessary for the state to be involved in a lot of economic decisions. Only when private choices—whether in education, the media, or the economy—contravene the common good should the state be involved. Ideally, the state should simply set up the system so that it's just not an option to do the kinds of things that are not consistent with the common good.

MW: That level of state intervention already happens in our current societies, where the state will disallow a merger between two corporations and things like that.

GJ: Yes, and frankly, I think that a lot of that regulation is probably unnecessary and wouldn't even happen in an ethnostate. A lot that's *said* to be in the public good really isn't in the public good today. But that doesn't disqualify the idea that there are public goods, there are common goods, and that the state should intervene in private affairs when private choices somehow negatively affect the common good.

In an ethnostate I honestly think there'd be probably less state control of the economy than we have today in America or Europe, because today a lot of state control of the economy is either private interests satisfying themselves at the expense of the public, or one group of the public mooching off another part of the public. The common good prohibits that. The only reason the state should intervene in private life is to protect the common good. Thus we should not tolerate factional governments where one group uses the state to exploit another. That is contrary to what Aristotle describes as the common good.

I look back to Aristotle's *Politics* as the model. Aristotle believed that a lawful, just society pursues the common good, and that unjust societies are characterized by factionalism wherein one group in a society—whether it's the majority or a minority or a dictator—rules for its own interests at the expense of the others.

MW: Question seven, and I'm not sure what Sargon was getting at with this question, but here it is: "Do the decisions of individual white people matter to the Alt Right's goals?" And I guess you could say: "Do the individual decisions of white people matter to the ethnostate's goals?"

GJ: Right. I think that this is just a very poorly formulated classical liberal question. It has the same underlying premise as the previous questions. All of this is pretty much liberal in its underlying assumptions. "Do the decisions of individual white people matter to the Alt Right's goals?" What I think he's getting at is: "Would we say that your individual decisions don't matter, and you're not going to get your way, on some occasions if that's what's required to create an ethnostate?" And the answer is "of course."

The whole point is that we believe it is right for the state to say "no" to private interests and decisions whenever those conflict with the common good. When those things don't conflict with the common good, or are neutral regarding the common good, then the state has no interest in them.

But we're not radical individualists; we're not libertarians; we don't think that if it's voluntary it's okay and that the state has no right to intervene. The state has the right and the obligation to intervene when private choices have negative consequences for the public as a whole.

MW: That brings us up to a question that I would just add in here, since it's crucial to Sargon's whole thing. You're saying that the individual is less important than the collective.

GJ: Yes, definitely. When the two conflict, the individual is less important than the collective. Do we save the human race or do we save one person, when forced to choose? Obviously, there's greater value in the collective than there is in any individual.

MW: Right, okay. I think that's something that he would

probe. He would ask you lots of little questions surrounding that like "What if the individual's a genius?" and "Should every individual's freedom not come before the well-being of the state, and the collective, the group?"

GJ: Yes, well, we could quibble about lots of stuff. I understand that's how he argues. But yes, I would definitely say that the well-being of the whole always trumps the well-being of individuals if there's a conflict between the two.

The greater good outweighs the lesser good, and the idea that every individual—every drug addict and junkie, every starving African child, or whatever—is of somehow infinite worth compared to the collective of mankind is absurd. How is it that if every individual has infinite worth, then when you add all these individuals up into a collective, that somehow has less worth, less moral standing than the individuals that you're aggregating together? It doesn't make any sense by any kind of moral arithmetic that I can comprehend. Radical individualism, the idea that somehow individuals have infinite worth, and that collectives don't have worth *qua* collectives, simply doesn't make sense.

Individuals die, but the race can go on. The race can be eternal. The things that we value will go on if we have progeny, if we have a race that survives us. Therefore, the idea that individualism is the be-all and end-all, is just silly. It's silly to think that something private and fleeting and subjective has greater worth than things that persist longer over time and that can be, in principle, eternal, and that are common.

We're all very wedded to our own subjective feelings. But in the end, we're all going to die, and we must come to grips with that fact and realize that the things that are most important to us have to be more important than our own lives. But that can only be the case if there are future generations to carry these things forward. Then you conclude that your individual life doesn't mean as much as the life of the collective. Which is why it's possible for people to sacrifice their lives for their families and their societies. That really is the enlightened attitude.

Individualism is a childish attitude. It's quite natural for children to be self-centered. They need to be cultivated so that they recognize that the world is bigger than them, and that things that are bigger than them—that endow their lives with meaning, and will carry on the things that are meaningful to them in the future—are more important, ultimately, than their survival. Especially because we're not going to live forever. Those who think that they can live a little longer or better at the expense of the social whole, it's not a very good deal, because really our only possible immortality is through the continuation of our people.

MW: Alright, moving on to the final question, question eight: "Should women have a role in public life?"

GJ: Yes, women should have a role in public life. However, I think that we have to be real here and recognize that if we are going to restore the biological integrity of our race—preserve our race as a distinct population—that includes also upholding healthy sexual norms.

The healthy norm is that men are protectors and providers. Therefore the public realm—the political realm, the realm of protection, and also the economic realm, the realm of provision—is going to be more of a male thing.

Whereas the norm is for women to be nurturers, which means that the private realm—including civic organizations, educational organizations, health care organizations—are going to be more feminine.

Therefore, if we really go with rather than against the grain of nature, we'll find that women will naturally cluster in the private realm. They'll be more interested in having kids. They'll be more interested in careers that involve nurturing: education, nursing, charitable work, etc. But those impinge on the political realm. The heads of charities play very important roles. Also, we must recognize that just because we uphold the norms doesn't mean that everyone's normal.

MW: Yes, I said this as well when I was answering it in the livestream I did with him a few days ago. I said, obviously there are always going to be outliers, and any healthy society should be able to accommodate those.

GJ: Exactly. An unhealthy society basically says that the outlier somehow has to be the norm, or there can be no norms because there are a few people who don't fit them. But that's folly. Instead, we should uphold the norms, and we should also make a certain amount of provision for the fact that some people don't fit them. That means that there are going to be women who, for whatever reason, aren't cut out for child-rearing but are talented in public life.

Now I don't like the idea of women in the military. I think that's stupid. Women should not be in the military. They should be involved in other things where they can do public service if they wish to do that, most definitely. There would be some female politicians. There would be female leaders of organizations that represent women's interests and children's interests, etc.

So yes, women should have a role in public life, although I think that in a healthy society that follows nature, public life would be primarily a male thing, because men are more drawn to public life. They're more drawn to the role of protectors and providers, and there's nothing wrong with that.

But just as there might be some men who are more drawn towards things like education, or roles that are more nurturing, there might be women who are more drawn to politics, and we can make room for them, because if we keep our norms straight and we don't get this misty-eyed, NAXALTy, sentimental, dumb form of individualism that's so powerful in our society, the presence of these people isn't a threat. It's not a threat to have the occasional woman in politics, or the occasional guy who wants to be a nurse instead of being a doctor.

People who buck the norms are not a threat as long as we don't have foolish, liberal attitudes, the kind of attitudes that we have today, where the existence of an outlier somehow refutes the existence of the norm. That's the NAXALT fallacy. Not all Xs are like that. There are outliers, therefore, there can't be norms. Because there are two ends to the bell curve, that refutes the existence of the great big swell in the middle.

But though women should have a role in public life, they're

probably not going to have as much of a role in public life as men. Thus we should not have the idea that there should be parity between the sexes in politics. Right now there is a widespread attitude that the movement is defective if there isn't a woman in every other seat at the American Renaissance conference. Years ago, Michael Walker, who is a very sensible guy in many ways, gave a talk at American Renaissance, and he said "I'd like to come here and see a woman in every other chair."

MW: What the hell? This is very strange.

GJ: I thought to myself, "This isn't ballroom dancing; this is politics," and chances are, there's never going to be a woman in every other chair, because this is politics. However, if we want to have a healthy community—if we think of the movement as not just a political thing, but as a new community, as a new order, as the seed of a new kind of society—obviously, we're going to want to have gender parity in that context. But in political organizations, it's not natural; it's not something you would expect.

However, if there are women who are contributing, and are doing good things, move over and let them in, and if there are men whose *only* contribution is to belittle women who are making active contributions, they need to be culled. I have no patience for that anymore.

MW: Okay, so in conclusion, what do you think about this survey, and what would you like Sargon's fans to know that they don't know?

GJ: Just judging on the underlying premises that are built into these arguments, the mentality that he's grandstanding towards is deeply liberal and individualistic, and that needs to be questioned. Liberal individualism is an essentially childish, immature, alienated form of consciousness, and we need to overcome it. We need to grow out of it, and that's what I would like to help Sargon's readers do.

Skepticism and relativism are just philosophical rationalizations for that deep solitude of the spirit, that selfishness, that individualism. But selfish individualism makes social life into hell. White Nationalists want to create a society that's better, that's healthier, that people feel at home in. To do that we have to fight against this deep solitude of the spirit, this skepticism, the selfishness, and this immaturity that I think is engineered today in our culture.

These people think that they're free and autonomous individuals. They've been engineered to think this way. They've been engineered to think this way ever since Thomas Hobbes, and John Locke and Baruch Spinoza and all the early modern philosophers started re-wiring the mind to create the modern individual.

The modern individual is not man as he comes from nature. He's a modern social artifact, and to be constituted as an individual is to be the artifact of processes that most individuals don't understand. But once you understand the processes that create this individualist consciousness, you realize you're not an individual at all. You are a product. You are a product of a particular education and a particular culture.

You might want to rebel against that, because ultimately, it's steering you on a trajectory towards a meaningless existence. It is a meaningless existence that is either actively conspiring with, or passively going along with, a program that will ultimately destroy Western civilization and the race that created it. You don't want to be a part of that. If you're serious, you don't want to be a part of that.

You don't want to lead a meaningless life and contribute to the downfall of one of the greatest civilizations and one of nature's masterpieces. You don't want to be like the people who allowed the ancient world to collapse into barbarism, who allowed the writings of Sophocles and so many others to perish. You don't want to be like the ancients who allowed civilization to crash, really irrevocably, because so little has survived of all the greatness of the ancient world. It really is one of the great tragedies of history. You don't want to contribute to that again.

That's what I want these people to start thinking about. That's what I implore them to start thinking about. Individualism is a trap. It's a false form of consciousness. It leads to a meaningless existence. And it is organically part of the process of the destruction of our civilization, which is being managed from above by people who hate us, and who want to replace us.

God knows what they want to replace us with. I don't know if they really have an endgame here. The endgame might be an image that Ayn Rand used in *Atlas Shrugged*, of a fat, Indian maharaja sticking a dagger into some toil-dazed wretch to steal a few grains of rice from him. It's some kind of dystopian global plantation economy. Low-tech, disease-ridden, and starved, where a tiny elite lord over a vast number of brown people. That's the endgame of the modern, globalist, liberal trajectory. Do you really want to contribute to that? That's a world that you have no place in.

MW: Okay, shall we leave it there?

GJ: Yes, let's leave it there. I think that's enough. That's some food for thought. So, Woes, thank you for suggesting we do this. I was going to just let this opportunity slip by because I'm just so damn busy.

MW: Yeah, well, this is why you've got to get onto YouTube and just do stuff like this. Because it's easier, it's quicker, and you did really well. That will reach people. That will convert people who would never go to *Counter-Currents* and would never read an essay, but they will listen to this while they're doing something else, and it will make them think.

GJ: Okay, great. Thank you so much

MW: Yeah, you're welcome.

GJ: Let's do this again.

Counter-Currents, July 24, 2019

Answering Normie Questions

Interview with JM[*]

GREG JOHNSON: I'm Greg Johnson, and welcome to *Counter-Currents Radio*. My guest today is JM, who runs the YouTube channel *NoMoreDogma*, and he's going to be asking me some questions. I'm not interviewing him. He's interviewing me.

So JM, tell me what you want to talk about.

JM: Okay. Thanks for having me on. It's the "normie questions" that I often get from people who may agree or disagree to a certain extent. But they have certain hang-ups with the overarching movement. If they find out that I'm involved, they say, "What about this? What about that?" Some of their questions are kind of tricky. I have the questions, and I thought you were a really good person to get the answers from.

GJ: Well, great. So let's begin.

JM: Okay. Here's the main one. Someone who agrees a little less often poses this one to me. They'll say something like, "Why are you proud of your country or people or culture, or anything like that? You didn't have any hand in building it, or have anything to do with its maintenance. So why are you attached to it?" I have my own answers, but this is why I wanted to ask you. You'd have a better answer. I get stumped on this one sometimes.

GJ: The basic response to that is very simple. It's based on the false premise that you are only allowed to feel proud of things that you have accomplished yourself, that you only have a right to things that you somehow created. And that's just not true.

---

[*] This *Counter-Currents Radio* interview was recorded in November of 2017. I want to thank Karl Thorburn for the transcript.

The simplest example of this is the concept of a gift. You don't have a right to receive a gift. It's given to you. It's handed to you. And you can take great pleasure in it.

I look at my race and my cultural heritage as a gift given to me by my ancestors. And I derive great pleasure and pride from that gift, because I look back on it and I see a lot of good things there. So if our ancestors bequeath us a superior culture, wonderful genes, interesting family lineages, and so forth, we can take pleasure in that, and it's ours. It's ours even though we didn't earn it.

Indeed, you can't really earn your cultural patrimony. There's nothing that we can give back to the past. They're dead and gone. We can thank our immediate ancestors, but we can't thank Mozart. We can't thank Euclid. The only thing we can do to thank these people is appreciate the things they've bequeathed to us and pass them on, pay them forward, to the next generation: making a next generation and giving that next generation an appreciation of the cultural patrimony that's been handed down to us.

So it's just not rational to say you can't have pride in things you don't earn. You don't earn the gifts that are given to you. That's what makes them gifts. But they are yours, you can take pride in them, you can take pleasure in them, and so forth.

And one of the things you can do, dialectically, to trip these people up, is ask them "If you don't think I have any right to take pride in things my ancestors have done, do you think I therefore don't have to feel any *shame* at what my ancestors have done?" Because the Left loves to speak out of both sides of their mouth on this kind of thing. They will throw out this very individualistic argument, "You don't have any right to take pride in the things you haven't done or created." But they are all too willing to hit you with the idea that you have unearned guilt and shame for things your ancestors did. And so, if they're consistent about this premise, you can get them there. If they really do believe you have unearned guilt, then why can't you have unearned pride?

JM: That's a good point.

GJ: This isn't my point. This is a point from Michael Polignano's piece at *Counter-Currents* called "White Pride and White Guilt." I think they're really powerful arguments. I'm always trotting these arguments out and hitting people with them. They really do get a lot of people to think.

JM: Yeah, that is really good. I'm always told about how I have this better standing in my society because of the history and my people and culture, but I had no hand in any of that, so how can I be proud of it? And like you said with the gift-giving, if I did have a gift passed down to me from my grandfather to my father to me, I would take care of that gift. I would treasure it and hope to pass it down one day. And basically play my role in that gift's saga.

GJ: And the kind of pride that you feel in this is not the kind of pride of somebody who's trying to take credit for someone else's work. It's like the pride that you feel in your children, your wife, your dog, or the things that are yours. It's natural to take pride not only in your achievements, but in the people that are connected to you.

And often that pride is not just an excuse to loll around and ride on other peoples' coattails. It's experienced by the best people as a command to rise to the occasion. Your ancestors achieved great things. The very least you could do is appreciate the great things they achieved and pass them on. So it's not a source of a kind of arrogance; it shouldn't be. It should be combined with a little bit of humility and gratitude. And that's what I feel towards the people that came before me. I feel humility and gratitude, and also pride, because they've done great things.

All those things fit together into, I think, the proper attitude that we should take towards our heritage. And that's a heritage that's cultural and genetic as well. Everything that's given to us by our ancestors — both our genes and culture — they should inspire a bit of humility, gratitude, and pride. And, therefore, a desire to pay them back with gratitude. But the really concrete thing we can do is to pay it forward, carry it forward into the next generation.

JM: Yes, that makes a lot of sense. That brings me to another question. As you were saying, having a culture and civilization, I would argue, that is one of the better ones in the world, leads to the claim of "white supremacy" being flung around. Is there any validity to that argument? That you're just a white supremacist, etc. I have my own response to this, but I'm curious how you'd respond.

GJ: First of all, we have to disambiguate what people mean by "white supremacy." Is it the idea that we believe white people are superior to all other groups across the board? That's obviously an untenable position. We're not superior to all other groups in all ways. For anyone to accuse us of believing that is almost accusing us of a straw man. Which is not to say that there aren't those who would argue that position. But I think they're fools to do that. They're on a fool's errand.

The other sense of white supremacy is the idea that we want to rule over the other races of the world. My answer is no, I don't want to do that. I don't want to live in societies with other races at all. That's what White Nationalism is about. We want to create ethnically homogenous societies in which we can feel at home. And that entails not having nonwhite populations that we have to dominate or lord over within our borders.

There are some problems with that. For instance, what do you do with little relict populations of tribal peoples, such as in the Amazon, the United States, Canada, Siberia? You give them ethnic reservations. You give them land. You give them the maximum possible autonomy over their internal affairs, and you leave it at that. But they're not going to have a foreign policy. They aren't going to have a seat in the United Nations.

So that's sort of a "white supremacist" position, but it's the least white supremacist position possible. It's certainly poles apart from the policies of the United States in the past where they tried to assimilate these people, teach them our language, try to get them to adopt Christianity, forget their native religions, customs, and so forth. I don't want to do that at all. I don't want to assimilate these people.

JM: Well, it doesn't work very well.

GJ: It doesn't help any of us. I want to keep our race and culture pure, and their race and culture pure. And that means separation and the maximum amount of sovereignty that we can extend to them.

JM: My take on that is keep the culture pure. These societies have institutions in them that have been built by Western European people, and those institutions are tailored to that group specifically. And I'm not surprised at all when I see that group performing well in those institutions, and other groups not performing well at all. You can see that the Western European people do well in all the institutions at an average or above-average level.

GJ: Well, we created this civilization. So it stands to reason we would be fairly good at living in it.

JM: That's where the supremacy argument comes from. I'm saying they have different values, a different culture. One that isn't conducive to our justice system, educational system, etc.

GJ: The way I put it, it's not some kind of radical cultural or moral relativism to say if you have size ten feet and you have to wear size nine shoes, you're not going to be comfortable. It's possible to say there are objective measurements, but some things fit you better than other things. They are relativized to your body. Your culture should fit you as well as your shoes fit you. Your institutions should fit you as well as your clothes.

The trouble with multiracial societies is they always start out being founded by a population that is not multiracial. Thus it has the stamp of the founding people. Thus any new people that come into that society are going to feel like it doesn't really fit. Sometimes they can fit in because they aren't so different to begin with. So they can assimilate, naturalize, and become part of the new system. We've absorbed many different European groups over the years, because Europeans aren't that fundamentally different from each other. But when you have blacks or Indians (to give examples from the United States), they don't fit. We've had blacks in North America practically as long as there have been whites, and they're still not integrated.

JM: Yeah. They have a very difficult time. And this bears out in every metric. It plays out exactly as you think it would each time. Crime statistics, SAT scores, credit scores. You know, all of these different ways.

GJ: Practically everything that we can measure indicates that blacks just find American civilization to be alien to them and alienating to them. It's not a good fit. And that's why they deserve their own kind of civilization where they're not constantly being forced to live up to standards that are alien to them.

The situation we have today is one that's guaranteed to create racial resentment. Because blacks resent being held to white standards, and whites resent blacks retarding civilization, lowering standards. And that's always going to be the case, because the peoples are just different. So if you want to have amicable, respectful relations with blacks, the easiest way to do that is to have separate societies, so they can live the way they want to and you don't have to live with them. You can live the way you want to. If you want to trade and exchange ballet troupes and buy one another's products and things like that, that's all well and good. But they should have their own homeland run by their own standards, and that's a good thing.

Another sense of white supremacy is related to this. When people talk about "white privilege," basically I say "Whites created this civilization. Therefore, it's natural that whites are going to flourish in it. If you want to call that white privilege, fine." The idea that white privilege is a bad thing assumes this argument that you don't have the right to things you don't earn. So we've been bequeathed this civilization by our ancestors that suits us, and we thrive in it. So sue me! I'm going to take full advantage of that. I'm going to rise and flourish in that context.

A related sense of white supremacism is this. I think white societies should be "normatively white." Meaning that we should uphold white standards in white societies. And we shouldn't apologize about that. Why shouldn't we be supreme in our own homes, in the societies that we create? If somebody comes to my home, he has to conform to the standards that I set, the norms that I set. I'm supreme in my own household.

I don't see why the French shouldn't be supreme in France, that they shouldn't uphold French norms in France. There's nothing imperialistic about that. It's just the natural behavior of people who are comfortable with who they are and proud of the way they are. The British should uphold their own norms. Or better: Scottish norms in Scotland, English norms in England, Welsh norms in Wales, and so forth. There's nothing wrong with that. That's completely normal.

A lot of kvetching and whining about white supremacy basically boils down to whites maintaining white standards in their own countries. And I do not think we should be at all apologetic about that. We should be militant about it if challenged. We should really push that point. There is nothing wrong with it at all. To that extent, I will defend white supremacism.

My ideal society is one that is only white. But even if we had simply and entirely white society in North America—say that there are no Indian reservations, etc.—say that you created a white ethnostate. We're still going to have travelers coming from abroad. Businessmen, tourists, and things like that. If you take a snapshot of the population day-to-day, there are still going to be something like 1% to 3% of the population who are not of the ethnic group that dominates it. We should not feel like that is somehow a fatal compromise with the principle of nationalism. That's just business as usual in any normal society.

The point where we would fail as ethnonationalists is when we start catering to outsiders by modifying our own standards. We should uphold the normative whiteness of whatever white society we are in. Swedes should uphold Swedish norms, Norwegians Norwegian norms. They should demand that people respect their customs, their way of life. People shouldn't come in and be the "ugly American" tourist. And, of course, the ugly American isn't anywhere nearly as ugly as the ugly Muslim in Europe.

JM: Yeah, you're right! And the thing is, it comes from morphing the cultural norms, and basically assimilates the norms to the group that's coming in. And as I was saying earlier, the institutions themselves, like you said, retarding them.

Dumbing them down, watering them down. Now it's not what it was before. And like you said, the host population can no longer flourish in the way they were able to do before. That's the line I have a big issue with. And as you said, I think there aren't many ways to control for that other than taking a look at these things and having a hard line on it, acknowledging this affects us.

GJ: Yes, the net result of catering to outsiders rather than having your own standards is that you've created a society where nobody feels at home. You no longer feel at home; they don't feel at home. And that's not any way to live.

JM: That's so correct. And on a personal level, I know what you mean when you say that.

GJ: When we go home to our house and close the door, we want to feel at home. But when we leave our house and go shopping, go to the post office, go to government buildings to sign deeds or whatever, we should also want to feel at home. We shouldn't be bombarded with alien languages, alien music, and feel like we're living in the *Star Wars* cantina all the time, except when you go back to your little home and close the door. Then you turn on the TV, and you're bombarded with the same multicultural crap too. That's no way to live.

All we're asking for is a country where we feel at home. That's not unfair in the least, because all these immigrants coming in have homelands that they're leaving. They feel perfectly at home there, and they try to replicate the things they like about their homeland in our country rather than assimilating. But of course we don't want them assimilating; we want them to leave. And we want them to be as alienated as possible, as long as possible, until whites get their acts together and start repatriating them. That's what I want.

JM: To me personally, what happened is, for such a long time things were implicitly of an American standard, or a white European standard. And that's just what people knew America as or Europe as. So they didn't mind letting these people in. And as it has started to change so much, it's started to affect them. And they are starting to notice these changes and say, "Hold on a second, wait." So now when I'm watching football, I have to see racial tension, things like that with the "take a knee" situation that happened recently. Anything like that really, with wage decreases, and so forth. And so we are starting to lose that, that implicit feeling. That feeling of implicit whiteness is starting to go away. I think that's the reason a lot of people are waking up to this.

GJ: I think the main things driving consciousness in our direction are objective changes in the multicultural system. We can't take credit for all the red-pilling that's going on. The system is doing that. Our job is to get memes out there to help people understand what's going on and also to create a political movement that captures and channels this new energy and consciousness towards positive change. We're not doing such a great job of that, but fortunately a lot of this is out of our hands. It's being driven by objective forces that the establishment can't control. And in fact, they are doubling down on it. So we have some time to get our act together, and we are slowly learning things and improving.

There's a fourth sense of white supremacy I want to deal with, and that is this question: Okay, Greg, say that you get your world of ethnostates. Say that there's Africa for Africans, Asia for Asians, European countries for all the different European ethnic groups. What about things like global ecological issues?" Pollution, stuff like that. We know that left to their own devices, and surely armed with Western technology and medicine and so forth, that the countries of Africa are undergoing population explosions, killing wildlife, devastating their environments. And that's going to have knock-on effects over here. We're not so isolated. We cannot confine global warming (if that's even a thing) to somebody's borders. So there are global problems, and issues of global welfare that have to be addressed globally. And the people who care about that are white people, preeminently. Are we going to stop caring about these things?

My answer is no. We are going to continue caring about these things, basically in the same way we do today. We're going to create institutions, and we'll have all kinds of blandishments to Third World countries to try to halt environmental degradation, halt population explosions, stop refugees from moving *en masse* to the United States and Europe. We're going to have to do these things. That means that yes, these countries aren't going to have 100% sovereignty. Because their pollution, refugees, plastic that washes out to the ocean, don't stay in their borders.

So there will be global institutions and initiatives like that, and whites will take a leading role in them, because we are the people who care about the planet. And if we don't care about it, the planet will be devastated. So we do have to take that into consideration. And that is a kind of "white supremacism." Every environmentalist, everybody who talks about "global solutions to global problems" is implicitly a white supremacist, because it's only white people who really care about these things.

JM: That seems to be how it is now, even. The people that go to those summits and whatnot, they're mainly European countries that are involved and European people who go to Third World countries to come up with solutions. It wouldn't be a huge change from how we currently deal with international problems. These countries would still be able to get together amicably. A lot of those other countries are currently running under a fairly ethnostate-esque situation. It really seems to be the Western European and North American nations that are dealing with the multiculturalism problem. The other countries are sticking to their guns, and they're still functioning just fine. So I'm not even sure it would be a leap to say it would be a problem dealing with these issues.

GJ: Right, Japan is an ethnostate. The Koreas are ethnostates. China is an empire, but it's normatively Chinese. And yes, to some extent these countries take part in international initiatives to try to deal with certain problems. Of course, the Chinese are huge contributors to these pollution problems, unfortunately. But maybe they'll start to grow out of that, when they start dying *en masse* from their own exhalations. Unfortunately they could lose quite a lot of people and it would actually improve the place. Fifty years ago, practically every state in Europe was an ethnostate. And they managed to cooperate with each other. There were the League of Nations, United Nations, NATO, the Warsaw Pact; all these different things were possible. Poland is 90%+ Polish. It's an ethnostate, and yet it's part of the EU; they can cooperate. So there's no reason to think that ethnically homogeneous societies can't engage in international cooperation, because they do it all the time, and they did it all the time.

JM: And that's what confuses me sometimes. Look back decades, not even centuries. That's what we had. Our laws were written in that way to say this is what we have, a white country, and European nation. It's only recently, because of mass transportation, that we've had so many nonwhites moving in. It's an unheard of idea to say we don't like that.

GJ: But mass transportation also allows them to move out, so that's a double-edged sword. And we'll start wielding it to our advantage, eventually.

You don't have to look too far back: From 1790 to 1965 we had immigration and naturalization laws that were committed to maintaining a white supermajority and a normative whiteness of America. That's within the lifetime of many people who are alive today. It's not so alien. And those institutions can be restored and perfected.

JM: The blueprints are there. It's not a far-off idea. It's within living memory, and people treat it like "Oh my God, what are you talking about? How dare you!" It really shouldn't be a controversial conversation or opinion. And it's treated like it's the most evil thing.

GJ: Right. I remember years ago, Scott McConnell, one of the publishers at the *American Conservative*, who's married to a Chinese woman, said "It's not inconceivable that a majority nonwhite United States could be a high-functioning society," and I wrote a letter to them, or posted it on their website, and I said, "There's every reason to think that a majority nonwhite America will not work, because we have majority nonwhite cities in America that don't work. We have Detroit or Camden, New Jersey."

A lot of people will say, "We can conceive of a future that's rosy and multicultural. But we can't conceive of a homogeneous society." Well, I'm sorry, but that's just rubbish. Because right now we have multicultural dystopias, majority nonwhite dystopias and hellholes all over America and all over Europe. Malmö, Sweden, is now nearly half nonwhite. We've got Detroit, Camden, all these black cities in the US.

And we've got concrete evidence of ethnostates working all around the world. We've got Japan. Singapore is multiracial, but it's normatively Chinese. And it was created as a way of getting the Chinese out of Malaysia. So those are great examples. We have Poland. Poland is a *de facto* white ethnostate. There are a number of countries in Europe today that are still overwhelmingly homogeneous and highly functional. I feel more at home in Poland than I do in large swaths of the United States.

JM: Really? That would be interesting, because those places you're talking about, even in America—Detroit, Charlotte, east LA, places like that—they're often talked about as being Third World places inside America. We've seen that problem for a long time now. That's kind of what led me to thinking of these questions. I've spoken to people who've seen this very same problem, and then they'll debate me or even get angry with me when I say, "Yeah, but there seems to be a very clear difference between that and the suburbs of Detroit, let's say, that function very well." It's kind of baffling at how hard that is to discuss.

GJ: When somebody says, "This is all America!" they're being disingenuous, because then you ask them, "Well, if this is all America, why don't you live in downtown Detroit? Why are you in the suburbs? Why are you not living in Camden? The property is cheaper there, and it's still America." They're being disingenuous; they're lying.

JM: Even the hardest, far-Left liberals live in places that are 95% white. Why is that? It's a natural thing for you to do. I wouldn't expect anything else.

GJ: Yeah, it's mighty white of them. I don't blame them for that. The only thing I blame them for is their hypocrisy. I'm glad in a way, though, that they're hypocrites, because it would be worse if they practiced what they preached. Hypocrisy is vice's tribute to virtue, as La Rochefoucauld said.

We need to get these people in touch with their real feelings. One of the best things Kevin MacDonald ever wrote was a paper called "Psychology and White Ethnocentrism,"[1] which surveys research about implicit bias, implicit racism, and shows that there's a lot to it. It makes sense in terms of the way the brain is wired. We are hardwired to be ethnocentric, and our cultural norms sit on top of a deeper brain that's hardwired to be ethnocentric. And when we talk about what we believe, oftentimes we will say things like, "There's one race, the human race," but in terms of peoples' actual feelings, and when they act on their sincere feelings, you see ethnocentric behavior.

So we need to get people to be more authentic. We need to get our people to act in a way that's consistent with their deepest feelings. And if we live in a way that's consistent with our deepest feelings, our nature, we are going to be happier.

One implication of MacDonald's research is that liberal multiculturalist types are not as happy as racially conscious people, because they are living in constant conflict with their deeper ethnocentric feelings. Whereas ethnocentric whites are fine with those feelings and accept them. Therefore, they aren't fighting against themselves. And if you're not fighting against yourself, you have a healthier psyche. You have more energy, a more positive outlook on life.

JM: Yeah, I believe that. What I notice about the harder Left is they have that *tabula rasa* viewpoint that it's all engrained, education, propaganda, whatever we have been taught since being toddlers. And the conservative says, "No, it's a bit of nature; it's a bit of nurture, environment, and so forth," and that was a relieving moment for me when I realized this isn't something to feel bad about. This is just a thing that I notice. I feel it. It doesn't change who I am. But I can now be open about this being the

---

[1] Kevin MacDonald, "Psychology and White Ethnocentrism," in *Cultural Insurrections: Essays on Western-Civilization, Jewish Influence, & Anti-Semitism* (Atlanta: The Occidental Press, 2007).

reality that I live in. I see it around me. I feel it within myself. And it's freeing to come to that realization. I remember that moment. It was relieving.

GJ: I think it was Sam Francis in the early 2000s who made the point that multicultural attitudes about race and ethnocentrism are analogous to Victorian attitudes about sex, assuming that the picture we have of the Victorians is correct, namely that they were very uptight, prudish, sexual hypocrites. Leftists criticize the Victorians saying: "You're making yourself neurotic; you're too uptight; you need to loosen up; you need to get in touch with your feelings, enjoy life, etc." So it is quite amusing to see Leftists engaged in the same kind of Victorian pearl-clutching, signaling, and hypocrisy when people talk about race. It really sets them up for a lot of mockery. Victorianism was eventually laughed out of existence.

JM: Yeah, that is an interesting analogy.

GJ: It points to a way of fighting this. Victorianism was mocked and parodied until people retreated from it. Its defenders retreated or went silent. It would be interesting to study the campaign against Victorian sexual mores to see if we can adopt some of its techniques for mocking and rolling back false consciousness and rank moralistic hypocrisy about race and multiculturalism. Our innate ethnocentrism is being suppressed just as much as our sex drives were being suppressed (supposedly).

JM: And it's just one of those natural feelings that you're going to have, and you're going to work against it as much as you can, but I imagine it came out in some really odd ways, if everything is to be believed.

GJ: Yeah. Jack the Ripper. People say, "Jack the Ripper is just what you'd expect in a society that prudish!" But the fact he was killing prostitutes means that there *were* prostitutes. So it wasn't that prudish when you get right down to it, but never mind. I think it would be an interesting project—you *Counter-Currents* writers out there, start taking notes!—look at the people in the Bloomsbury set who were combatting Victorian norms. One of the things they did was write scathing little portraits of eminent Victorian hypocrites and prudes. I think that we should start doing that ourselves, creating vivid portraits of our ghastly hypocritical elite. The Tim Wises of the world.

JM: And there are plenty of them.

GJ: A guy in my Facebook feed is constantly coming up with tweets from Jews where on the one hand they're talking about "My fellow white people, we need to repent for our racism" and then in another tweet, "As a Jew, I am a strong supporter of Israel." At a certain point "fellow white person" is going to become a meme for dissembling Jew.

JM: I've seen that a lot myself, and I wonder if that's something that's done on purpose or if that's really some sort of self-deceit. On one hand it's so blatant and on the other it's just tricky.

GJ: Right. I want to write an essay, or do a photo essay where I just collect all these tweets and call it something like "fellow white people," just to document this Jewish meme. Because I do think it is a very conscious thing. It's the "Dress British and think Yiddish" kind of dual ethics that they inculcate into themselves.

JM: Well, it could definitely become a meme. The new Fellow White People.

GJ: We could definitely mock that quite effectively. This guy has been putting together a really good dossier of tweets documenting this. Some of them are just howlingly funny, too. I think mocking the hypocritical Victorian-style repression of our natural ethnocentrism is a really good route forward in breaking the whole of this false consciousness for our people.

JM: I totally agree. I've looked at social identity theory. It's not a controversial theory. And it's usually talked about in different ways. So for instance, a punk kid—a kid who listens to punk music and has torn-up jeans—is going to gravitate toward other punk kids. But this also pertains to race. We see it in classrooms, cafeterias, jails, housing developments, and really every way that it could possibly be borne out where they don't force diversity into a workplace, for instance. Yet we see that the people in those situations, especially the white people, are often talking about how tolerant they are, and how evil it is that the money they make is built on the backs of slavery, all those tropes. They are doing the same thing they criticize everybody else for. It is better to have the hypocrisy than it is to have them moving in and trying to solve it.

GJ: So are there more questions on your list?

JM: A random white person doesn't care about me in any meaningful way. At the same time, how would I deal with someone who's a minority, and we've been friends for a long time? I understand all these ideals, but I have this minority friend. So the question for the everyday person, in daily life. Do you understand what I'm saying with that?

GJ: There's a very simple answer to this question, and it's actually quite widely applicable to these issues: to recognize that traits are distributed on bell curves. That means there are going to be outliers, exceptions in every group. So it's going to be possible, indeed inevitable, that you will meet members of other racial groups who are outliers, and who are therefore highly compatible with you.

The first person I ever knew who was an advocate of eugenics was a white guy that I met years ago. He probably had an IQ in the 90s and was a total sports fanatic. He believed it would be best if he married a black woman so he could sire a brood of superior basketball players.

JM: (laughing)

GJ: I was just appalled at that. But that was the first eugenicist I ever met in real life! Here's a below-average IQ white guy, and that means there are going to be a lot of people in the black community that will be at the same level as him. They have the same interests in sports and the like. So he found that he had a lot in common with blacks, because he was an outlier in the white population, and overlapped with a significant portion of the black population.

There are very bright blacks. I've had a couple of black students when I was teaching in the past, who were really very bright people. They saw right through my bullshit. They were probably smarter than me. So that's just a reality.

But we have to recognize that social trends are founded upon not the outliers and the exceptions, but the vast bulk of people in that huge bulge of the middle of the bell curve. So it might be possible for exceptional blacks and normal whites to get on well together and work together. It's totally possible.

But when you are making policies, you look at the averages. And when you put the white average and the black average side by side, there's a huge difference. The bell curves just don't line up, and not just in terms of intelligence, which has huge implications for all areas of life, from the number of traffic accidents you get into to the number of unplanned pregnancies to the number of crimes you commit. Intelligence is not the only factor, but it's so powerfully predictive of social outcomes it might as well be the only factor.

JM: Yes. It really is.

GJ: Richard Lynn has pointed this out. He recognizes that there's more to being a human being than your IQ score. But in terms of predicting social outcomes, it's as if you could pretty much neglect all these other things.

We also could measure differences in personality that are not connected to intelligence, like levels of sociopathy or empathy, impulsiveness, attitudes toward time and responsibility, etc. Those bell curves don't match up with the different races, either. So there's bound to be conflict when you put these groups together, because the averages, which are the great number of people in society, do not coincide, even though the outliers might coincide.

JM: There's something we see when we radically change immigration policy. All of these negatives come out of it. I would call it catastrophic. And this is happening. Even though there might be white and Muslim neighbors who get along fine and have dinner with each other and are great friends—that's wonderful. But on a larger scale this is causing a lot of problems, and the policy should be built around "What is happening most often?" The average here is that most often this is not working. So if we separate, it might really stink that those outlier relationships won't happen anymore, but in terms of a healthy society and a healthy culture, the policy might have to go against somebody's personal liking, I guess you could say.

GJ: The common good has to trump individual interests where they conflict. That's what I believe. And to try to turn everything into sentimental tales about your lovely friendship with this exceptional black person, that's just rubbish. That's sentimental claptrap to obscure reality and choke off sensible policies with a veil of tears and sob stories. We just have to plug our ears to these sob stories, like *Romeo and Juliet*. Frankly, the parents were right! When your two families hate each other and have a long history of murdering each other, it's not a good match. It won't work well. There's no happy ending there. And yet we seem to think that "because Shakespeare" we've got to dismantle all the miscegenation laws. That's sentimental folly. And we have to be stronger and say "No!"

The principle that the common good trumps individual interests should be honored and upheld. Not sneakily imposed whenever we have to. Which is what happens in liberal societies. Liberal societies are constantly imposing costs on people for liberalism. Yet at the same time, when they trot out their moral principles it's all individualism, this exceptional person here, how dare you get in the way of this doctor from Guatemala who just wants to be part of the American dream, etc.

I've got a whole file of "Things that never happened" stories. Leftists love to come up with these stories. I'll bet they're all made up. There's one story where a French workman comes to a Muslim family's home. He looks at a picture on the wall of some bearded character. He probably thinks he is some sort of imam. He asks, "Who's that?" And the Muslim woman of the house says, "That's Victor Hugo!" And the whole point is to show that this Frenchman was undeserving of his cultural patrimony, and this Muslim had more right to be in France than he did because she appreciated Victor Hugo. Well, that's rubbish. France is his birthright, which is not contingent on anything, and she is an alien, no matter what her identity papers say. I'm sure it never actually happened, but they love to spin these stories out.

JM: Yeah, they'll show Jimmy Kimmel on the street asking "Who's the vice president?" and have some drunken college girl who doesn't know the answer. That doesn't have anything to do with the larger point of us having a civilization.

GJ: They love these kinds of tales. There's a term called NAXALT, which stands for "Not all Xs are like that." It's always trotted out whenever you try to make arguments about groups. It's basically just a corrosive form of brick-stupid individualism, usually coated with lots of sugar. It's supposed to paralyze thoughts about groups. I have an essay that I'm rather proud of called "In Defense of Prejudice." It's basically a defense of inductive generalizations, and also a critique of NAXALTing, meaning trying to make policy based on outliers rather than averages. NAXALTing is especially common with women for some reason. The idea that you can find an exception to any rule, which means we should just stop making generalizations and just sort of dissolve into tears and sentimentality and "Every sperm is sacred; every Mexican is different" kind of nonsense. It is basically put out there to paralyze rational thinking about policy.

JM: I can see that being a female trait.

GJ: We simply have to call bullshit on it whenever we hear it. We have to mercilessly mock it. It's fine to just say, "Look, we know there are exceptions. But we're making policies for the whole society, and we believe the common good trumps individual interests whenever they conflict. And that means you might have to give up your precious black friend." And just watch the steam coming out of their ears, because you've stopped the bullshit in its tracks.

They're not in a position to argue that the common good should trump individual interests when they conflict. Of course, they have a long list of occasions where they will trot that principle out, *ad hoc*, of course. It's always done *ad hoc* by liberals, because they will never just affirm it as the central principle, because then so much of their bullshit would be on the chopping block.

JM: Going back to your *Romeo and Juliet* point, I think if that were to be written today, the ending would be that they live, fall in love, and their families grow closer together, get along swimmingly, happily ever after.

GJ: The Gounod opera actually adds a happy ending to it. It was done in the nineteenth century. I guess progress had sufficiently infected thinking, so they realized, "We need to write a happy ending to this."

JM: One of the things that really infuriates me is people willing to toss out tradition, history, heritage, as if they don't matter. "Why do you care that you're white? Why do you care about your culture, history, country?" Any of those questions. It seems very common sense to me that this is my group, my culture, my family. I don't know why I should ever have to defend that. And in so many conversations I do. I don't understand how it even becomes controversial to begin with.

GJ: Right. You can get to a of people by following this kind of argument: "You have a son or daughter. Little Johnny, for instance. Little Johnny is yours; he looks like you; you love him, etc. But he's not the brightest kid on the block. And you're putting aside money for his college education. But little Johnny might not be as smart as little Akbar down the street. So why are you paying for Johnny's education rather than Akbar's education?" And people will get really upset if you try to pull that on them. They feel like they're being bullied. But in terms of the norms they've accepted it's hard for them to answer it. This is why we're losing everything, because we don't have good answers to arguments like that.

But the proper answer is, "Because he's *mine*. He's *my* son. And if I don't take care of my son, nobody else is going to take care of him. You want me to take care of Akbar down the street, but his parents aren't going to take care of little Johnny." So we need to take care of our own, and love our own. And it's natural, normal, and right to love our own.

You can apply that more broadly than to just your immediate family. It's natural, normal, and right to have preferences for people who are like you. And there's a whole body of psychological theory that is very well grounded empirically and very powerful in its predictive ability. This is Genetic Similarity Theory.

It turns out that animals, even incredibly primitive animals, animals that don't even have brains, very limited creatures still have a little unit built into them that allows them to sort between kin and non-kin, and they prefer kin. Ants: they're not big-brained creatures, but they still prefer kin to non-kin, and this is essential to life.

JM: Yes. And I would think that the party often most against this, being liberal, atheistic, secular, therefore believing in evolution and things like that, they should understand this is buried fairly deep in our brain. This isn't the prefrontal cortex at work here. And you see the outcomes all the time. And the hypocrisy of the people who use their prefrontal cortex to argue against it, but in practice live as naturally as anybody else, according to their group preference. And this is not going away anytime soon. I think some people have a sort of accelerationist way of dealing with that, thinking "Well, let's just mix together. Soon everybody will be beige."

GJ: Well, when they say that, I just say: "So you recognize that diversity doesn't work. And you want to commit genocide on all the distinct peoples of the world so you can make diversity work." I've got a better idea. Instead of committing genocide, why don't we just put the brakes on all the mixing and start unmixing things? Wouldn't that be nice? When you get a liberal saying, "We've got to have one beige race," they've given the game away. It is great to get liberals on record: You liberals now recognize that diversity is a curse, and you are willing to engage in genocide in order to create a workable monoracial, monocultural society.

JM: And oftentimes, talking out of both sides of their mouths, they'll get into some kind of cultural appropriation. So they're not in favor of the mixing on one hand. But when it comes to race they'll say, "No, we have to get through this and make everyone just one human race."

GJ: Right, if you observe their behavior, or get them a little drunk, you'll see they are totally uncomfortable with nonwhites unless nonwhites are outliers totally assimilated to upper-middle-class white norms. They are very uncomfortable around people who aren't like them. So really, their model is cultural genocide for everybody else.

JM: I've seen this plenty of times in my own life. Get them a little drunk, and it really starts to shine through. "That's extremism, collectivism, tribalism!" all the bad words commonly thrown against it. The people who argue against it also act that way and notice the same thing. It's not a matter of trying to force this into anybody. It's just about bringing it out, letting them express natural feelings.

GJ: Yes, and this is one of the reasons I'm fundamentally optimistic about our cause, because I believe that nature is on our side. There are never going to be any workable long-term good consequences of doubling down on multiculturalism. They're not going to get their coffee-colored humanity. There will be outliers who will miscegenate, but the bulk of people will not. The most ethnocentric people will reproduce their kind, and the least ethnocentric people will disappear, and therefore whites are going to become more ethnocentric on average, because miscegenation is going to pick off the people who aren't ethnocentric. Whites are going to become more pro-natal on average, because birth control, miscegenation, and feminism are going to take anti-natal people out of the gene pool. So you're going to find a tendency towards greater ethnocentrism and pro-natal attitudes on the part of white people. Now, I do believe white genocide is possible, but they'll just have to kill us. We're not going to willingly mix ourselves into oblivion, or just cease to reproduce.

So what's going to happen is increased ethnocentrism and racial polarization. Eventually, if we don't manage to persuade these people to do the rational thing, and halt these horrible policies, they will be halted by systemic collapse; they'll be reversed by bloody wars and conquests.

We want to avoid that by enlightening people, by making them realize this is not going to end well, and then instituting sane, peaceful, and humanitarian solutions, just to reverse the trends. We've had fifty years of demographic decline for whites in North America. If we reversed all those trends, if we put things on the right path for fifty years, we would be fine.

I never tire of saying we would reap a lot of the psychological benefits well before those fifty years are up. Because we would feel as a group that we've got a future again. I think one of the reasons there's so much nihilism, helplessness, drug addiction, decadence, and decline among white people is because deep down white people don't believe that we have a future. We need to give our race a future again. And if we resolve today that we are going to have a future, we are going to start feeling the benefits of that today. Even if it takes us fifty years to have an ethnostate, we will start reaping the benefits of it today, and if we reap the benefits of it today, that will hasten the day the ethnostate actually arrives.

JM: The resolve will lift peoples' spirits, give them a purpose, give them something to work toward. Taking that gift and cherishing it. Preparing it to pass on to the future generations. So it's very enlightening.

GJ: Even though selfishness is constantly preached in our societies, people are happier when they feel like they are serving a greater good. Unfortunately the greater good the Left is preaching is just nihilism and self-annihilation for white people. The greater good that we are advocating is preserving our people and all the other peoples of the world. And carrying our heritage on, and raising it to new heights. That's what we stand for. That's a truly inspiring vision, and that's something that can make peoples' lives a lot more meaningful than playing video games, watching porn, watching sports, and all the other forms of nihilistic self-indulgence society has to offer, basically as a way to while away our time to extinction.

JM: Yes, I agree, and like you said it is getting worse, the opiate epidemic and things like that. They are out of hand, and have been for quite some time. It is purposelessness, and I've been in a debate on social media recently about lacking purpose and what that means. It's interesting. Human beings seem to have a drive for that, and we don't seem to have one right now. I shouldn't say "we," because I feel like I do, and a lot of others do. But I think as a group we don't. And we are seeing that. And if that idea were to come, we would start seeing the effects of it right away.

People will bring up problems within specific groups like the Alt Right. And I think what you and I have been talking about here is bigger than that, more than that one singular movement, it's about a group of ideals, values, a culture. Some people agree with a lot of ideas or believe in the ideals that we are talking about, but they don't have a problem with certain groups, but I think as long as you agree and believe in that, hopefully you'll be making the right decisions.

GJ: Right. We need to change peoples' consciousness, and the right political leaders will come along. Once there is a sufficient change of consciousness, a lot of people with leadership skills, money, and organizational skills will pop up and carry that forward in the political realm. Therefore you don't have to commit yourself to any of the things that are in the offing today.

I agree that there's a great deal of dissatisfaction. Since Charlottesville a lot of people have gone silent in social media. I feel that many of our people are hanging back and watching because they don't like what they're seeing. And after the Shelbyville event this past weekend there has been an explosion of bickering and infighting about this. People have had enough of these marches and events like that. They feel like it's not the right way forward.

We need a vehicle to carry this consciousness forward in the political realm, but we haven't figured that out yet. But I'm not worried, because the people who have gone silent and who are biding their time aren't going to change into multiculturalists. This is an irreversible change. No one goes back from this. No one who sincerely sees what we see and believes what we believe ever goes back from it.

There are apostates. I've written an essay called "The Psychology of Apostasy." But these are people who believe this stuff, or thought they believed it, said they believed it out of social reasons, not because of actual convictions that these are truths.

But those who see the truth of this aren't going to leave for some other thing. They're just going to wait for a better vehicle to come along. We've got time. We've got decades to turn this around. I truly believe that. The longer it takes, the harder it's going to be. But we do have decades to turn this around. So I don't think we need to hop onto any kind of premature political populist bandwagon. A lot of us aren't. A lot of us are simply biding our time and waiting and watching.

But as long as we continue to articulate the changes that people are experiencing because of the baked-in problems of multiculturalism, they're going to come to us. They're going to mill around. They'll become a huge crowd. They'll eventually become a significant enough minority that they can tip the whole balance of society in our direction. Then we're going to see rapid political change. I think it will be so rapid, so sudden, and so total that we will all be shocked. It will be as shocking as when communism fell in 1989. And I believe it's going to happen in my lifetime.

JM: Once you actually understand the idea, I don't think there's any going back. And it's a big reason I've been a huge fan of *Counter-Currents*. I don't think you're trying to tout yourselves as something you're not. You're putting out these ideas, giving people a place to go, and I think it really is a place people should check out as a way to understand things better, like where some of this velocity comes from, what are some historical events and tactics that we can look at and learn from. And for those who are biding their time it's a perfect place, and even for those who want to make their voices heard, it's a place they can become educated. I think you've done a great job of putting that together.

GJ: Well, thank you very much; that's music to my ears!

We've been going on for about ninety minutes now, so I think we should wrap up. Are there any last thoughts before we go?

JM: No, that was great, thank you very much.

GJ: Well, let's do this again. Write down some more questions for normies and you can bounce them off me. Honestly, we should be doing more of this, because we've got to get our talking points down. And this is a good kind of workshop. It's good for me, too. So let's make plans to do it again.

JM: Absolutely. Will do!

Counter-Currents, August 7, 12, 13, & 14, 2019

Vanity, Pretentiousness, & Snobbery

A Conversation with
Hugh MacDonald*

Greg Johnson: I'm Greg Johnson. Welcome to *Counter-Currents Radio*. I'm going to have another conversation today with Canadian filmmaker Hugh MacDonald. This is actually based on a conversation we had quite spontaneously in London earlier this month. We walked around Hyde Park one afternoon, and the topics of vanity, pretentiousness, and snobbery came up, and he had a really challenging take on these things, and it really got me thinking about these topics as well. So anyway, Hugh, welcome to the show, and let's just have a conversation.

Hugh MacDonald: Awesome, thank you. We are thinking about vanity, and the words came to my mind that vanity is a virtue. You know, we think of it as something that should be looked down upon as a hated quality, but I think vanity can be a virtue. I really think a lot about Jack Donovan's concept of honor and honor being caring what other people think of you.

GJ: Right.

HM: And caring how you are presented to the world and caring about how you look is a positive thing. That's what it means to have honor, appreciating how you are presenting yourself.

GJ: Right, and yet vanity is traditionally regarded as a vice, and a lot of people regard it as a vice. So, I guess really we need to unravel the senses in which vanity is a good thing and in which vanity is a bad thing, because I'm sure we can all think of

---

* This *Counter-Currents Radio* conversation took place in the spring of 2015. I want to thank KC for the transcript.

bad examples of vanity, if we put our minds to it. So, what's the difference between good vanity and bad vanity? What's your concept of good vanity? Can you just sort of summarize it in a nutshell?

HM: Well, first, let me deal with bad vanity, because I think it would help us define it better. If I think you were to look up a definition of vanity, it would say something like caring too much about how you look or how you are presented. And I think anything that is too much, by definition, is bad. So, if you define vanity in that way, it makes it difficult to turn it into a good thing. Caring too much about how you are presented.

GJ: Right, right. So, I'm looking online. Excessive pride in one's appearance, qualities, abilities, achievements, etc. Character or quality of being vain or conceited.

HM: So, calling it excessive. I guess it's a kind of checkmate if they say excessive. But I guess the question is, what is excessive? If a girl is constantly posting pictures of herself, of her makeup, on Instagram, or a guy who is a bodybuilder is also posting pictures of himself and flexing his muscles, people will say, "They're so vain. They're always so concerned with how they look." But I think that it's not necessarily such a bad thing, the practice of doing those things, because they're both art forms. It's art in two ways. It's art in the sense that putting on the makeup in the first place is an art form, in and of itself, and then taking the picture of yourself is another layer on top of that, and arguably, even, perhaps, it's not as in depth an art form, but the face you make is almost like acting—like kabuki, Japanese theater.

GJ: I am the most unphotogenic person in the world, and I know there is an art to being photographed, and I just don't know it. I don't know how to do it. I always have these horrible expressions, or the wrong posture, or whatever. So, yeah, there is something that people who are photogenic do, over and above looking good, so that they actually take good pictures. I know plenty of photogenic people, and I know unphotogenic people, and if you take objective measurements of their looks, they might actually be fairly similar, but one person is really hated by the camera, and the camera loves the other. So, they're doing something. There's some difference there. There's some factor there.

Other definitions of vanity are lack of real value, hollowness, worthlessness, and something worthless, trivial, or pointless. So yeah, it's really being freighted with intrinsically negative aspects. But, let's just try and focus on what's positive in vanity: a person trying to make himself or herself beautiful. There's nothing wrong with that as far as I can tell. There's nothing wrong with the attempt to beautify the self to whatever extent that's possible. And if somebody is born beautiful, he can still do things to present himself well or badly. If some people are born ill-favored, they can still do something to make themselves look good or not. They can dress well. They can carry themselves well and so forth. I think that is not objectionable in the least, and we're just talking about appearances. I think it's good to try and be as beautiful, as attractive, as dignified in appearance as possible. Would you agree with that?

HM: Yeah, I might even go so far as to say it's our responsibility to do our best to look as presentable, to look as good as possible, especially from a collectivist, nationalist perspective. I think a lot about it when I visit Europe, and I see people in the subway, and they're so well-dressed compared to Americans and North Americans. I am in Canada. And I think about why is it that Europeans dress so well as compared to Americans? And I think part of it is because this idea of responsibility of presenting yourself well comes from a collectivist perspective. You're not just representing yourself as an individual, you're representing your people. So, there's that weight, there's that responsibility on your shoulders. I think about why the Europeans dress better. I think it's partly because you have all these European countries that are very small and so close to each other, and it's so easy to travel across borders. If you see a German sitting on a bus, and he's poorly dressed, you look at him and you think, "Oh, Germans, they don't dress very well." Or if you're visiting someone else's country, and you see the way they dress, you can say, "Oh, those Italians, they don't dress very well." And, so it inspires this competitiveness, the competitive feeling between countries, that they need to present yourself well. It's a feeling of national pride.

GJ: Right, it forces you to up your game a bit. Yeah, I think there's some truth to that, and I think that if we are a nationalist movement and we want to promote nationalist values, especially since we are so marginalized in other ways, that we should be attentive to how well we present ourselves so not only do we have the best arguments, but we put out the best books and the best videos and we look really cool and we are just a formidable group of people that should be taken seriously. I think that's something that we should all aspire to.

HM: Yes. I live in Toronto, the motto of which is "diversity our strength." It's often referred to as the most multicultural city in the world. It's not the most ethnically diverse, but that's just a piece of propaganda that said Toronto is the most multicultural city in the world. I am constantly surrounded by people from every other part of the world, and when I see a white person who is poorly dressed, a fellow European, I think, "What are you doing? You're making us look bad."

GJ: You're letting down the team.

HM: You're letting down the team. It's not so unacceptable if you live in some completely homogeneous all-white area, because you're not a representative of your group. People just look at you as an individual. I think that's part of the reason why people in small towns, they don't dress as well, because they don't have to. They're all just individuals there. Whereas when you thrust people into a multicultural environment, we all become representatives of our group. And so in that sense, it's your responsibility to present yourself well, because it's not just yourself you're representing, it's all of us.

GJ: Yeah, that's a good idea. I like that. So, the good sense of vanity I think that we can come up with here is the idea that vanity is praiseworthy because it is praiseworthy to try and present yourself as well as possible. You should try and look as good as possible. Beauty is a value. Beauty is an objective value in the world, and there are things you can do to make yourself more or less beautiful, just as an individual. And yes, there's also this collective dimension to it. We're representing our group, and within our movement we're representing certain ideas, not just our group, and we should aspire to look good. We should aspire to present ourselves well. And there's nothing wrong with that. I think that's actually good.

So why, then, does vanity have negative traits? Well, one of the ways I think that vanity has a negative connotation is it's not really talking about vanity so much as the *failure* of vanity, the failure to actually make oneself look good. For instance, think of an example of a woman who has put on a lot of makeup and looks grotesque. She looks like she's painted up for kabuki or something like that. There's a line around her face where the skin tone changes because she's painted her face one color and doesn't blend naturally with the rest of her skin, or she's garish, and people say, "Ugh vanity! Vanity, thy name be woman!" But what's really being objected to there is not actually her ambition to beautify herself. It's the failure of that ambition. She's failed to beautify herself. And I would go even so far to say that at the core of the horror is that we realize that she can't really be objective about her appearance. She's deluded about her appearance. She thinks that looks good, and so there's a sense of falsehood about it. There's a sense of falsehood, and there's a sense of failure, and those are things that I think are built into the negative connotations of vanity. And that's why some of these definitions include that sense: the lack of real value, hollowness, worthlessness, being trivial or pointless, as in it was a vain effort.

HM: Or like to take the Lord's name in vain.

GJ: Right, right. The lack of value, the hollowness, the worthlessness aspect of it, I think, is captured when you look at somebody who has failed to beautify herself, and actually looks grotesque, and you wonder, "How could she not know this? How could she be so deluded?" And so I would say that vanity is not a bad thing if it actually results in the objective beautification of the self, and that the objectionable sense of vanity is simply a failure of real vanity. Does that make sense?

HM: Yeah, and so would that appropriately be referred to as pretentiousness?

GJ: Yeah that's an interesting question.

We also got into the question of pretentiousness when we were walking around Hyde Park. I think pretentiousness always has a negative connotation, but I think that one can actually say that there is a positive connotation of pretense in this sense: if one is trying to, say, improve one's tastes or improve one's knowledge.

Now, let's just talk about taste. Vanity has everything to do with the beautification of yourself and maybe your things. Your car is an extension of yourself, your clothes, whatever. *Taste* is your susceptibility to the beauty that's out there in the world. Taste is the faculty of being receptive to beauty and able to enjoy beauty. And it's a faculty that can be developed. And because it can be developed, and because it requires effort, sometimes you are stretching beyond yourself. You're trying to transcend your level of taste at any given time so you can appreciate greater beauty or deeper beauty. And when you're doing that, there's an element of what you can call pretentiousness to that.

Let's talk about the opera or classical music. That is one of the classic examples of something people think is pretentious. Why do people think it's pretentious? Well, on some level what they're saying is that if they went to the opera or to a classical concert, they would be pretentious because it's "not them." It's not the kind of thing they enjoy. They'd feel like they were acting or putting on a show.

However, I would argue that no one ever becomes better without, in a sense, pretentiousness. Because there's real beauty, there's real value in classical music or opera. And if you're going to appreciate that, you're going to have to stretch yourself. You're going to have to go there; you're going to have to sit there; you're going to have to listen to it. You're going to have to try. And yes, there's a whole stretch of time where you might feel like a fraud sitting there and clapping. "I don't know what's going on. I lost track of what is going on. But I'll clap anyway because everyone else is clapping." That kind of thing. You feel like a fraud, but if you do that long enough, and you expose yourself to these things of real value, you're not going to be a fraud anymore, because you're going to actually come to see real beauty that exists out there, and you're going to have expanded your taste. So, pretentiousness in that sense can be defined as a kind of ambition to improve one's tastes, just like vanity can be the ambition to improve one's appearance. And I don't think there's anything wrong with that.

Now the question is: "What's the bad form of pretentiousness?" Well, I think it's probably analogous to the bad form of vanity. A bad kind of pretentiousness would be somebody merely pretending all the way through and never actually growing. They're just engaged in a kind of fraud, and why would they be engaged in this kind of fraud? Well, maybe they're gratifying their need for social approval. They're pretending to be a connoisseur of something because they're trying to impress other people.

A friend of mine married a very prominent author. I won't name any names. Anyway, he was a big gourmand. He had a lot of money coming in, and he wanted to improve himself, and so he became very pretentious. He went around attending operas and symphonies and eating in fine restaurants and things like that. And one day someone fed him some cat food as paté, just to see whether he would spit it out in disgust or whether he would pretend like it was delicious. I won't even tell what happened. But if he pretended it was delicious, that would be a sign of pretentiousness in the bad sense: if somebody is just pretending to enjoy certain things because he wants to fit in with a social set or be thought of as highfalutin, superior, and sophisticated.

HM: Sounds like Leftists.

GJ: Well, yeah, a lot of these people are that way, and that's one of the things that's so disappointing about the Left, because there used to be Leftists who were really principled people, formidable people. They had arguments, they had ideas, they had commitment. I don't see many people like that anymore. But I see a lot of really hollow people who are just pretending to believe certain things as a way of gaining status within a thoroughly corrupt system.

But back to pretentiousness. What's really objectionable about bad pretentiousness is not that it's an attempt to become better than one actually is. It's actually faking it and not really trying to become better. So, the objectionableness of bad pretentiousness is really the fakery, not the ambition of becoming better.

HM: Sounds like Leftists, eh? I guess part of the rejection of pretentiousness is because there's this element of trying to say, "I'm better than you. I'm above you." To be pretentious is almost a form of oppression. It's a way of saying, "I'm above you, and you're beneath me." Just like a Leftist urban elf who gets upset if you say, "Oh, that's so gay," and they get very excited about it, and they say, "Oh, you're not supposed to say that. I'm very offended that you said that." The way a Leftist pretends to be offended by things. That's pretentiousness. And why are they doing it? They're doing it because it gives them social status. It puts them in a position of power where they can look down on you and talk down to you.

GJ: Right, but is what's offensive about that the fact that they think that they're better—or the fact that they're fake? I reject egalitarianism. I really do think that some people are better than others. So, I don't have any objection to snobbery. Snobbery is another concept we talked about, and it fits in with this very well. People think that being a snob is a terrible thing. They look down their noses at snobs, which is a kind of snobbery in itself. Being a snob is looking down on people, thinking you're better than others, thinking certain things are better than others. But if we are anti-egalitarians, then we have to defend snobbery in some sense, because snobbery is just anti-egalitarianism in practice.

If you are an anti-egalitarian, there are certain things that you won't do; there are certain things you won't eat; there are certain places you won't be; there are certain people you will not associate with; and to do so is to lower yourself, because these things are beneath you. I think that if there are real hierarchies of value, then snobbery is an absolutely important thing, because it is a manifestation of seeing those real hierarchies in value.

And again, the objectionable sense of snobbery for me is not that people are making distinctions of quality, but that they're making distinctions of quality based on false criteria. So, if a person thinks that he's better than somebody else just because he makes more money, or because he's got the latest iPhone, or "Her shoes are so 2013," that kind of stuff: I look down on that. That's false snobbery. That's fake snobbery or merely conventional snobbery. There are all kinds of distinctions of quality that people make in the world based on being up-to-date and being fashionable that don't necessarily track real distinctions of quality in the world, and if people get their sense of worth caught up in false criteria of quality, then they are snobs in the bad sense. But again, what's objectionable is not making distinctions of quality. The objectionable thing is making distinctions of quality based on false criteria.

So, I think there is a danger on the Right, when we look at liberals and we look at Leftists and we see how pretentious they are, how snobbish they are, how elitist they are, to think, "Oh well, we're populists; we're against pretentiousness and snobbery and elitism. We're just all a bunch of slovenly bozos here." And we shouldn't do that, because what's really objectionable is not aspirations to be beautiful or aspirations to have better tastes or aspirations to make real distinctions of quality. What's objectionable is making those on false criteria, false premises. What's objectionable about the Left is not that they are elitists but that their elitism is based on false criteria, and it's also sort of false to itself, because they claim that they're anti-elitists and that they are egalitarian. So, there's a kind of bad faith there. There's a hypocrisy there.

HM: Yeah, I guess elitism is the positive way of saying pretentiousness. If you're a Rightist, elitism is a positive quality.

I first started realizing that I was an elitist when I would wake up at 5:30 in the morning to go to the university swimming pool, and I'd always feel better than others when I was the first person at the pool, because it made me feel I'm tougher, and I'm stronger, and I'm more disciplined. And as people would slowly trickle into the pool, I'd look down on them, and I'd think, "I'm better than you. I'm more disciplined than you. I woke up earlier than you. I took the harder path than you did." And that's what it means to be better.

And then some days I'd accidentally sleep in. The worst thing, the really bad thing, is when you *choose* to sleep in. And then I'd arrive at the pool a little later, and people were already there, and I'd hate myself for it. I'd feel like "Aw, I'm not as disciplined today. There are people who are better than me today." And that's when I first started reading about elitism and then realized, "Oh yeah, I guess I'm an elitist."

If you can think that you're better than people, or realize that people are better than you, and look down on people for their weaknesses, that's elitism. And I think it's interesting being an elitist. It reinforces itself. You become better by being an elitist. You come to value strengths more and you look down on weaknesses more. The reason why I'd look down on those people who came in late to the pool is because I see in them the weakness that I see in myself.

GJ: Exactly. The core of elitism, the thing that makes it justified, is that the true elitist is really hardest on himself. When you despise your own weakness, you despise your own laziness, you despise your own lack of knowledge, you are a tough critic of your own performance, and things like that, you feel licensed to be critical of others, too.

HM: Right, and on an outward level, it can appear like it's hatred of that external individual. But on a deeper level it's not really hatred of that individual; it's a hatred of the weaknesses in that individual. And on an even deeper level, it's just a hatred of your own weaknesses. I can see that if you see this other guy, who woke up late that morning, and you look at him, and you think, "Ugh, that's disgusting. I hate the weakness that I see in you," it's because really you are aware of that weakness in yourself. It sounds like a Buddhist expression—maybe it is—that the world we perceive is a reflection of ourselves.

GJ: Right, right.

HM: Elitism makes you better because it makes you strive to be strong, and you hate weakness in yourself, and you hate weakness around you. And so that's not pretentiousness because it's not fake.

GJ: Yeah, or you could say that it is pretentiousness in the good sense. Pretense has a sense of acting. But there is a sense in which self-improvement involves acting, for instance, when you are learning how to play the piano, or you're learning to have certain virtues. Actually, the best example comes from Aristotle. Aristotle talks about it this way. The way to acquire virtues is to act virtuous, to do the sort of things that virtuous men do. But one is not yet virtuous, one is just imitating virtuous people. One's being pretentious, in other words.

But there comes a point when, if you practice long enough, it is no longer a kind of mechanical imitation of an exemplar. It becomes second nature. It becomes you. It sinks in and dyes the very fabric of your soul. It becomes deeply habituated rather than something that's just superficial, that you're going through the motions of. That's true with playing the piano or learning any other kind of skill. At first, there's a kind of mechanicalness to it, where you're just going through the motions. You're imitating others. Then, at a certain point, when it becomes fully internalized, suddenly the performance is coming from within you, rather than coming from you watching somebody else and following along with what they're doing. And at that point, you have become the person that you were pretending to be.

I think that kind of pretentiousness is just a normal part of moral education, or practical education, including one's tastes very broadly speaking, and what's bad about pretentiousness is that a person might never go beyond that. They might always just be acting or always just be imitating; it's never become fully internalized; it's never really become them; it's just a kind of inauthentic copying or mimicking or performance, perhaps because it doesn't matter to them to be real.

This, I think, gets into a whole dimension of psychology that's really interesting and kind of perilous, too, which is the concept of narcissism.

When people talk about vanity, another term that they'll use is narcissism. "So-and-so is very narcissistic." Again, I think that there's a certain sense of narcissism that's not a bad thing. The myth of Narcissus is that he's captivated by his own reflection in the water. He exists as a prisoner of his own image, reflected in something external. Now, that is a bad situation. That is to be empty, in some sense. The bad sense of narcissism, as I understand it, is when a person's sense of worth is entirely dependent upon how he or she is perceived by others, such that it's just good enough to manipulate how others perceive you in order for you to feel good about yourself. So, a narcissistic person doesn't necessarily have to be virtuous, doesn't necessarily have to have good taste, doesn't necessarily have to *be* anything. He just has to *seem* that way well enough that others *think* he's that way, and then he derives a kind of gratification from the reflection of himself in the eyes of others.

What's objectionable about bad narcissism is the inauthenticity, the unrealness. The narcissist isn't necessarily *really* a good person, or *really* a smart person, or *really* an accomplished person. His primary concern is to be *seen* that way, so he ends up manipulating other people—defrauding other people of esteem, basically. Narcissists get esteemed for things they're not, and to do that they have to manipulate how other people think. So it's a parasitic, manipulative form of life. I think that's a really negative and dangerous thing.

Another sense in which people talk about narcissism is self-love. A certain amount of that, I think, is crucial. But then there's a sense of narcissism as basically being empty and unreal as a human being and living in the perceptions of others, so that you're false, manipulative, and dependent on others. But at the same time, it's possible for there to be an element of narcissism, an element of imitation, an element of acting, an element of playing to the crowd in the process of growth and maturation. Boys want to be like their dads. Women and girls want to be like their moms. You want to have certain features of the people that you respect. You want to internalize those features, and so there's a great deal of psychological development that just works through the process of imitating others.

How do you know you're doing a good job? They tell you you're doing a good job. So you're imitating others in order to gain their accolades, in order to gain their praise. The problem, though, is when you never get beyond that, and it never becomes authentic. It never becomes you. It never becomes real. So you're always just acting, always just playing a game. And then beyond that, there are the people whose whole lives are involved in manipulating others so that they praise you, or they think well of you, or they give you things. That's a kind of fraudulent existence. It's a bad existence because it doesn't require you to be real, to have real virtues and talents. And it also makes you entirely dependent on others and manipulative of others rather than being somewhat psychologically independent and capable of grappling with the problems of life on your own.

In his book *Émile*, and in his *Discourse on the Sciences and Arts* and *Discourse on the Origin of Inequality*, Rousseau claims that the main problem of civilization is vanity (*amour-propre*). He has a very negative sense of vanity, and it's basically just narcissistic manipulation of others in order to gain esteem and status. He thinks vanity is at the root of human inequality, in the bad sense of human inequality, human unhappiness, tyranny and domination, and so forth. He thinks vanity is really the root of all social evils.

But Rousseau thinks that the solution to these social evils is self-love (*amour de soi-même*). So, he makes a contrast between vanity and self-love, and he thinks that self-love is grounded ultimately in a sense of being able to master the challenges of life, whereas vanity is ultimately haunted by a kind of emptiness and a kind of dependency on other people. The man with self-love has the power to conquer nature and control nature, whereas the man who lacks self-love and whose life is caught up in vanity lacks the power to conquer nature, and therefore he has to conquer or manipulate other people in order to deal with the problems of life.

Rousseau wrote his book *Émile, or On Education*, basically because he was trying to figure out how vanity becomes a problem. He thinks it becomes a problem because of maleducation starting from the very earliest phases of life. So he tries to put forward an alternative scheme of education that allows people to gain self-worth and self-love rather than vanity. The aim is to create a society of people who are self-actualized and self-confident, not psychologically dependent and manipulative. It's a society of autonomous adults who are capable of non-manipulative, non-dependent relationships with one another. And he also says that the product of this education would basically be a kind of *Übermensch*—of course he doesn't use that term. A few people with this sort of education who have self-love but lack vanity, and thus have inner strength rather than weakness, could smash the world. This is a chilling and powerful idea. He really was trying to create an *Übermensch* who could revolutionize and overturn a society of weak, manipulative, vain, dependent, narcissistic people.

HM: To aspire to be good and to aspire to make yourself better, that's a positive quality.

GJ: I would say so.

HM: And to care what other people think of you is also a positive quality. That's also a healthy thing, because it encourages you to improve.

GJ: Yes.

HM: But if you have that care without the actual self-improvement, that's when it becomes unhealthy. If you care to present yourself as something that you're not as a form of lying, that's the bad thing.

GJ: Yeah, exactly. And so there's a sense in which honor is a good thing. What is an honorable man? He's a person who is concerned about his reputation, for instance.

HM: And the reputation for his people.

GJ: No man is an island. He's not just an individual.

HM: That's how Jack Donovan in *The Way of Men* frames honor. Honor is important, because you are a representative of your group, and if you're acting like a fool, you're making everyone else in the group—your whole tribe—appear weak.

GJ: Yeah, and it's not just *appearing* weak, although that's part of it, it's to *make them weak*. And that's really the most pressing concern. We want appearances and concerns with appearances ultimately to track what's real. And if you behave in a bad way, if you're the kind of person who's flagrantly unconcerned with honor, if you're the sort of person who doesn't care about his reputation, if you're the sort of person who therefore breaks promises, or speaks in an impulsive way, or just does dumb stuff, that doesn't just make your group *look* bad, that *makes your group weak*.

HM: It makes your group bad.

GJ: It makes your group bad, not to mention looking bad.

HM: It's not just looking bad. It makes you bad.

GJ: Looking bad is the alarm bell. That's what we see. But the real concern is actually making us *be* bad. And there might be some times when you have to be unconcerned with looking bad in order to be strong. Can you think of examples where you might have to look bad in order to be strong or effective?

HM: It could be empowering to make it appear as if you don't care what people think of you. Yeah. And you can deliberately kind of force that appearance. You want people to believe you don't care what they think because, if you don't care what they think of you, then they don't have power over you.

GJ: Yes.

HM: You're stronger if you genuinely don't care what they think of you, so it's to your advantage to at least *appear* like you don't care. In public spaces, I've heard this many times. People will be very vocal about saying, "I don't care what anyone thinks of me. I just don't care what people think." But if they honestly didn't care what other people thought of them, then why would they bother to vocalize that idea in the first place?

GJ: That's a very good point.

HM: You know people will tell you that they don't care what you think of them, because they really care. They care that you know that, because it's an empowering thing. If someone else cares what I think of him, then I have power over him, because I've got some pull. He fears my judgment. So, it's important at least to present yourself as if you don't care while secretly caring. You obviously really care, which is why you do your best to appear like you don't care.

GJ: Right, right. Vanity—being too concerned with what other people think of you—comes off as weakness to me. However, you don't want to be so "strong" that you don't really care at all what anybody thinks of you. Because then you're autistic, or you're like Aristotle's God, who's sort of autistic. Aristotle has this notion of God as totally self-absorbed and uninterested in anything else: totally self-contained. The Daoists have a similar idea of the sage or the emperor as entirely self-contained. He doesn't even need to act, because others are drawn to imitate him.

Now, there's something real about that. There's something deep and true and powerful about that. I think that really psychologically strong and healthy people do have a kind of self-containedness and aloofness about them that makes them very charismatic. However, if they were entirely that way, they wouldn't even be human. But if you're a person of real quality, then you can't really seriously care about what everybody thinks of you—just anybody, right? Because most people don't even have the criteria to judge.

HM: Right.

GJ: If you are a skilled violinist or a physicist, if you are somebody who does something that is very difficult and very hard to appreciate, the number of people whose opinions really matter to you has to be pretty small. You're only going to be concerned with the opinions of your peers, the people who are in your class. So there might be people who are superlative individuals, extremely strong people, extremely self-contained people, and they might look like they don't care about what anybody thinks, but they're still human, and they still care about the opinions of significant others, people who matter to them; the opinions of the people who matter to them, matter to them a great deal. If they didn't, they wouldn't even be human. They'd be on an entirely different plane of existence.

When you believe in hierarchy, when you believe in inequality, you're going to naturally and necessarily believe that there will be certain people who are so advanced that they don't really care about the opinions of most people. And therefore, they are going to have this quality of aloofness and self-containedness that can be extremely attractive, extremely charismatic. Yet, they do have peers, and the opinions of their peers do matter to them, because they're human, and because there are other people on their level. It might be lonely at the top, but there are still other people at the top. But the opinions of everybody don't necessarily matter.

No matter how important you are or how accomplished you are, you're still a human being. You still put your pants on one leg at a time. So on some level, there's going to be a sense in which anybody can judge you. And on those levels where anybody can judge you, then their opinions will matter. You might be the hottest guy in town, you might be the smartest guy in town, you might be really up there, but if you get out of the car and slip and fall in the mud, you're going to look bad to anybody. You're going to feel embarrassed, no matter who sees you, because there are certain levels in which we're all the same, basically.

But still, on some higher levels of achievement—moral, intellectual, aesthetic, scientific—the opinions of others that really matter to you become very rarefied, and the numbers of people who really matter become quite small. Therefore, you seem distant and almost godlike to a lot of people.

It's fashionable for people to say, "I don't care what other people think of me," and it fits in with a sort of corrosive individualism in our culture. However, if people really don't care what other people think of them, they're kind of dangerous. They're not quite human in that sense. That's something to be concerned about.

HM: Especially if they're an ally, because they're part of the same group. When someone is weaker than you, then it doesn't matter what they think because they are no threat to you.

GJ: Right.

HM: That's the real importance of caring what other people think. If someone is potentially threatening, then you want to appear strong to them. You want to appear like you could resist them if they were to attack you. Whereas, if they're weak, even if you yourself appear weak, you still feel like you're stronger than them, and they want to attack you.

GJ: Right.

HM: I've been thinking a lot about what it means to be civilized. And if you think about an uncivilized people like sub-Saharan Africans, for thousands of years, they really didn't create very much. Whereas, if you compare them to a civilized people like Europeans, and you look at what all we did—our music, our philosophy, our buildings, our architecture, our science, our government, all of these things—we created so much. Creativity is really the distinguishing thing between being a civilized people and an uncivilized people.

And that's connected to the idea of vanity in a sense that fashion is a form of creation. A woman's makeup is a form of creation. I guess even bodybuilding is a form of creation. And so, there are people who look down on vanity, but I say: No, vanity is a positive quality. It's a form of being civilized; it's a form of cultivating yourself; it's a form of carving your existence into a form of self-expression. It's a form of making your existence a form of self-expression, carving every atom of your being into something. That's what a civilized person does; that's part of what it means to be civilized: it's to be making things, constantly making things, constantly creating things, constantly making art—art understood as that through which one can express oneself.

GJ: The most pretentious thing possible is to be civilized. I wish I had said this, but I think it actually came from Thomas Sowell: Every new generation is an invasion of barbarians, and you've got to civilize them, or they'll destroy your society. To a barbarian, there is nothing more pretentious than being civilized. And how have our people raised ourselves above barbarism? It's a pretense, if you will. Not an empty pretense, but an earnest pretense, an earnest pretense to improve oneself.

HM: And so to be vain, to take the time to very consciously present in your haircut or the clothing that you wear—these are in fact expressions of culture. Your hairstyle is a form of culture, and the way you speak even is a form of self-expression, and that's part of what it means to be cultured and to be civilized, which is an important part of what it means to be a European.

GJ: Yes, yes. Most of our people don't know it yet, but our people are in an ethnic struggle for their very existence. Those of us who are self-conscious of that existential threat, we need to really be at our best. We need to live up to the ambition that we set for ourselves, which is to be the people who preserve and carry forward civilization. That's a big task.

HM: The war that we're fighting is a culture war. Our cultural landscape is a battlefield, and so every act, every cultural gesture, the clothing that you wear, the way you cut your hair, the style in which you build your home, how you decorate your home—all these forms of self-expression: the music that you make, the art you paint—this isn't just window dressing. This is an act of war. This is an expression of our European identity and our rejection of multiculturalism: very consciously dressing in a traditional European style, wearing a European suit, or cutting your hair in the fascist style. It's an expression of our European identity, an act of war, a gesture of our rebellion and rejection of multiculturalism, and a celebration and embrace of our European identity and European culture. That's vanity, being very conscious about these things and how other people perceive you, and how you are presented. And so, in that sense, vanity is a virtue, a positive quality.

GJ: I would agree, and at the same time, we have to be aware that the negative sense of vanity makes us weak, but the positive sense of vanity is at the core of what makes us strong and how we become stronger and better.

The Left doesn't dismiss the idea that art and fashion are connected with politics. Our people tend to dismiss those ideas. It's part of the reactionary populism that a lot of our people just sort of stumble into because they really are just reacting against something they dislike about the Left, and therefore they want to negate it. They think that "Oh, these people are horrible elitists, so we're going to somehow be democratic ordinary Joes." But ordinary Joes don't beat elites. Elites beat elites. So we have to be a better elite than they are. That's the only way we're going to win.

But the enemy doesn't dismiss the inherently political nature of every aesthetic gesture, every bit of fashion, every bit of art. And we need to see things in the same way. They're right. Everything is politicized in that sense, and the reason they promote ugly hairstyles and ugly clothes and ugly music is to attack us. When people present ugly music as great art, we should feel the same sense of horror and existential threat that we feel toward somebody who throws acid in the face of a beautiful woman. It's the same malice; it's the same evil.

The flip side of having taste is that it makes it difficult to enjoy a lot of things. I can't listen to some kinds of singing—or "vocalizing"—anymore. But on the other hand, it does sensitize you to things that are threats and meant as threats to our identity, and I think that we all have to become more sensitive to that, because we really are under threat. And the threat comes in all directions.

HM: I can think of clear examples of degenerate art when it comes to film, especially films like *Bridesmaids* or *The Kingsmen*, which was a clear celebration of degeneracy. But anyway, that would be cool to have a separate broadcast talking about degenerate art versus quality art.

GJ: Yeah, that would be a really entertaining and interesting thing to dig into. Well, Hugh, we've been going on for about an hour now, and I really feel like this is becoming clearer to me. I really do think there are defensible senses of vanity, pretentiousness, and snobbery, which are terms that are used pejoratively. I also think we need to defend these things, because as European nationalists, we are anti-egalitarian. To defend the idea that there are real distinctions of quality in the world, we have to defend snobbery, which is the ability to distinguish between real levels of quality. We also have to distinguish between a good and a bad sense of pretentiousness. I think good pretentiousness is the ambition to improve oneself. And like you were saying, the good sense of vanity is an aspiration to improve oneself specifically in terms of one's beauty. These are all things we stand for and believe in. I think this was really valuable. I think it's probably very valuable for our listeners. So, let's definitely do this again soon.

HM: All right, sounds good.

Counter-Currents, July 9, 10, & 11, 2019

Conversation with a Philosopher[*]

INTERVIEWER: What is race? How would you define it as a philosopher?

GREG JOHNSON: Races are natural kinds. I believe that there are natural kinds in the world. I am a metaphysical realist. I think there is an external world, and the external world comes divided up into different kinds of things. Races are sub-species of the broader human race, and they are best described as inbred populations of the larger race that have undergone divergent evolution in particular environments and therefore have certain distinct characteristics that are evenly distributed throughout the group.

So, if a population of our ancestors became isolated in a particular environment, they might have new traits emerge. These may then be selected for. And because members of the population breed with one another, these traits would become uniform throughout the population. Given enough time, enough divergent evolution, these different races can become entirely different species in the sense that they can't breed with, communicate with, or even live alongside other kin that have diverged from them.

I think of race as a natural kind that has emerged through divergent evolution. As divergent evolution continues to ramify you don't just get different races but you get radically different groups. There was a time when human beings and lobsters diverged on the great tree of evolution. Obviously we don't get along too well together. We can't have amicable human-lobster societies. If we spend too much time together, they end up in pots of boiling water.

---

[*] This *Counter-Currents Radio* conversation with a professional philosopher was recorded in January of 2018. I want to thank Julien Prail for the transcript.

I: You actually cleared up quite a few questions I had on that. Let's imagine that we had a white ethnostate, and let's imagine it as a single white ethnostate, so we don't have to get bogged down in national states and all that. Would it be conceivable in such a situation that eventually, a few thousand years down the line, you would have a divergent evolution within the group "white people" such that they can't live side by side.

GJ: Yes, in fact we have examples of that, because not only is human evolution biological, it's also cultural. We have layered cultural evolution on top of biological evolution. Culture is a new way that we can grapple with the world, and it undergoes selection pressures in the same way that biological traits do, and it's much more mutable and replicable; ideas can change and spread much more quickly than genes, whereas genes might take generations to spread through a group.

We do know, for instance, that even white groups that are genetically very similar but have diverged in terms of their cultural evolution cannot get along very well with one another. The Irish and the British, the Serbs and the Croatians, the Czechs and the Slovaks: these peoples are very close to one another genetically, but some things set them apart so that when they live together in the same system, they fight and want to have their own spaces.

I: Would it be fair to say that you are getting your understanding of race from science, or is it something else, such as the metaphysical?

GJ: I don't think it's primarily scientific or metaphysical. I think that race first and foremost is an observable phenomenon. We *see* racial differences, and that means that we are the kind of beings that are *capable* of seeing racial differences. Science and metaphysics can help us *understand* that process, but what is most real and ineradicable is the awareness of these differences that exist in the world and the fact that we are equipped to be aware of these differences and the implications of that awareness.

As we look more carefully and deliberately at our awareness

of differences, we discover just how deeply ingrained this is, and in fact, it's ingrained into evolution long before human beings were even close to appearing on this planet. It has a prehuman evolutionary heritage, the awarenesss of kinds, kith and kin. Ants are not big-brained creatures, but their tiny ant brains contain a module that allows them to distinguish between kin and non-kin. The evolutionary explanation for that is that genes seek to propagate themselves through time. They do that by seeking out genetically similar partners as vehicles for their propagation.

There is a whole body of scientific knowledge known as Genetic Similarity Theory that is extremely powerful in explaining things we already know through observation. Philippe Rushton, who was a friend of mine now deceased, a psychologist who wrote *Race, Evolution, and Behavior*, did a lot of research on Genetic Similarity Theory.

One of the things that he did research on was the question "Do opposites attract?," and the answer was simply "no." In fact, the basis of attraction was genetic similarity. He even found that we actually have modules in our brain that allow us to pair up with people who are genetically similar to us in ways that we are not even consciously aware.

One example he gave was histo-compatibility. We actually will find and partner up with people to whom we are histo-compatible (that is to say, we are not allergic to). Even though there is no conscious mechanism that we know of to produce that result. There are things in our brain that allow us to be aware of genetic similarities in other people that do not rise above the threshold of consciousness and that we don't even know how to explain yet.

When we look at the data, it is so powerful, it's so clear, that there are patterns of affiliation between people based on genetic similarity. It's going to take generations of scientific study to finally unravel the phenomenon. It explains families and politics; it explains why we have a stronger affiliation with our own kin than with our neighbors or people who are very different genetically speaking. It explains national and regional affiliations and so forth.

I think Genetic Similarity Theory is very important in getting to the causes of things, but again it all comes back to really explaining observable, categorizable historical experiences that we all have.

Therefore my answer to the people who argue that race is a social construct is: "No, it's not a social construct. There are race-based phenomena that we all observe, and if anything is socially constructed, it is the theories that come after the fact and explain what we are already seeing." What we are seeing is not socially constructed, however. What we are seeing is naturally provided. It is a given. The process of scientific understanding is a social practice. But that comes later. We can't completely absorb the *fact* of race into *attempts to interpret and understand* race.

I: To say that something is socially constructed doesn't imply that that thing is fake?

GJ: No, it doesn't. A society is a social construct, and society is real. The reason people want to argue that race is a social construct is they want to argue that it is *mutable* and can be changed. We can change our minds. We can change our social constructs. Therefore, social constructivism on race is basically a metaphysical presupposition of the egalitarian project. If we see that there are things that make people unequal, like race, IQ differences, psychological differences, and we construe them as social constructions, they are therefore mutable, and they can be changed over time. We see that social institutions and languages change over time, and that gives egalitarians the hope that race differences can be altered towards the norm of equality.

I: Wouldn't divergent evolution also imply mutability of race?

GJ: Yes, indeed. There is mutability on the genetic level, but race is not mutable in terms of the conventions we use to talk about it. Now the way that race can be mutated through conventions—and this is how convention feeds back into biology—is by instituting patterned breeding, eugenics or dysgenics. And every society institutes some kind of eugenic or dysgenic regime, whether it intends to or not. Every society based on its institutions, its values, and so forth, will lead certain kinds of traits and people to be prized and reproduce more than other kinds of traits and people. Therefore, culture does influence us on the genetic level by instituting selective breeding.

I: The reason I asked the original question on what is race and how you would define it is because I've been speaking to a lot of prominent White Nationalists and "Alt Right" figures, and when I spoke to Richard Spencer specifically he was very clear to me that his conception of race is not derived primarily or even secondarily from science. He actually spoke of race as a mystic might speak of God, if that makes any sense.

GJ: Well, what did he have to say?

I: Well, he said first of all that his conception of race was not drawn from science. I don't have his actual words in front of me, but he almost defined it negatively, like a negative theology. He was talking about it in terms of what race is not. I guess he also used some vague terminology, and maybe I'm misreading that as mysticism, but it was an interesting definition, and I think I'm seeing a lot of diversity on this very question, with White Nationalists that I've spoken to.

GJ: Richard Spencer has his own views on these things, and I can't really defend or attack them because they seem very vague to me. They seem half-baked. As I said, I would not characterize my view as being based on science. I think it's based on experience. It's based on observation. Science is one of those things that comes along behind and tries to explain and deepen our understanding of experience.

Now, metaphysical concepts inevitably come into play as well. I, for instance, am a realist. I believe that there is an objective world and that there really are objective natural kinds. They are not eternal as Aristotle thought objective natural kinds were. They are mutable, but they do exist, and it's a defensible position.

The first things are observation, experience, and common sense. Then come science and metaphysics to explain what we are seeing, deepen our understanding, and also perhaps give rise to useful predictions and prescriptions about prudent behavior if you're constructing a better society or a better business. What kind of things can we do to make society more functional, more harmonious, more happy, given the nature of race and given the nature of genetic similarity, genetic ties, genetic enmities, and so forth that exist?

I: Well there does seem to be, I've noticed, a sort of animosity towards scientific materialism within the White Nationalist side. Am I misreading something?

GJ: There are people who have an animosity to scientific materialism within our sphere. I'm not one of them. I am ultimately a materialist when it comes to science. Materialism is a metaphysical thesis that all that exists is matter in some sense. I wouldn't consider myself a materialist in that sense, but I would in the sense that a great deal of our understanding of the observable world around us is going to be in terms of cause and effect that exists on the material plane of existence, and to be dogmatically opposed to that and say, "There is a radical difference between man and nature, a radical difference between body and mind, between culture and biology," is a kind of obscurantist metaphysical presupposition, usually connected to certain religious beliefs, that actually stands in the way of us understanding how things really work.

For instance, there are a lot of people with the strong conviction that there is something called freedom of the will. I think that people make choices, but I do not think choices happen in accordance with what people call free will. The more I learn about genetics, the more I find that genetic determinism, which is a kind of materialism, is incredibly fine-grained. Most convincing are ample studies done with twins, identical twins and fraternal twins. The identical twin studies are the most exciting ones.

Twins who are raised apart, sometimes in very different households, end up having similarities in their tastes, in their life courses, even fine-grained similarities like the kind of cars that they drive, the kind of careers they have, the kinds of names that they give their children. It is really uncanny. When I first started reading this literature, it was kind of chilling.

You think there are things that are *me*, that are truly me, and this is my identity — things like my favorite foods and colors, my tastes, the kind of music I like — all of that is uniquely me. And it is uniquely you, if you're the only one with that genome in existence. But if there's another person with that identical genome, then lo and behold, he's going to like Mozart too.

The amount of similarity between people who are genetically identical is enormous, and it can't be explained with random luck, obviously. You also find that identical twins who live together and know one another, or even ones that meet when they are adults, have an amazing rapport; they understand one another's thoughts; they can complete one another's sentences; there is a kind of harmony that exists between these people that is really remarkable.

To me, one of the great problems of politics is creating a harmonious society: a society where people feel at home, where they can understand one another, communicate with one another, work together, accomplish things, where they don't fight, where they don't feel alienated. The ideal society in a way, the one that would be most harmonious, would be a society of identical twins. If we could all be cloned (of course it would have to be a male clone set and a female clone set), in the next generation all the kids in that second generation would as related to one another as brothers and sisters, and all the parents in that older generation would be as related to them as their own parents. It's a weird thought experiment, but that kind of society would be more harmonious based only on overwhelming genetic similarity than societies that are more genetically heterogeneous.

Now, if that is the case, then we have a model, a kind of platonic circle or form, of a group of people who can get along the best. Getting along may not be the only social virtue, but it's certainly one of the things that societies strive for. Even if people are unsociable, we want them to be unsociable in a social way, with Faustian strivings and all of that. We want that to be containable so it doesn't ruin society.

That is why diversity is a bad idea. If the most harmonious relationships between people are among those who are genetically identical, then with each increase in genetic diversity, there's going to be less harmony, less understanding, more propensity to fight, less propensity to cooperate, to accomplish great things, and eventually you're going to get so much diversity that there's simply no real community in the sense of people having something in common.

The only thing people might have in common in a maximally diverse society is that they trade with one another. It would be a community of people who have nothing in common. That's what the marketplace is, and it's the least common denominator way of people getting along. Even there, we've got to have common things like credit cards that work, a monetary system. So even there, we've got to have some things in common.

Although I think that's a rather dystopian picture of reality, because it's a world without any kind of sense of belonging; it's a world without any ability to work together to create glorious things, which are expressions of a particular people and their sense of destiny and identity. It's a world without a lot of things that we would recognize as high culture, adventure, progress, and so forth. That's a dystopian view.

The ethnostate is basically the idea of society where people enjoy the benefits of close genetic similarities, as well as a common language and a common culture. Therefore they can understand each other and work together and so forth. If you have a society like that—and they still exist in some places in the world today—they're worth keeping. They are worth improving upon. And they are worth creating. We want to share that blessing: the blessing of harmony and genetic and cultural homogeneity with as many different groups as possible. That's the whole project of ethnonationalism.

We want homelands for all distinct peoples. And once we create homelands for all distinct peoples and give them maximum autonomy to pursue life as they see fit, then we will see, I hope, peaceful divergent evolution in culture, and even in race, and the world will be a beautiful place. It is kind of a "Garden of Eden" in which the maximum variety of races and cultures coexist, each in their own place. It might not be a world where there's complete peace, because there's always going to be stuff to fight about, but it's going to be a world without civil wars, we hope, and it's going to be a world without empire building and a lot of the causes of quarrel that exist today.

I: You don't think there would be an increase in warfare between states at that point?

GJ: I think that if we can create an ethos that recognizes the value of ethnic self-determination for all peoples, that is a better way of getting rid of warfare than the idea of trying to put everybody together under some kind of global government, which is the idea pushed by the League of Nations, the United Nations, the EU, and all of the globalist institutions. They've explicitly said that if we have continental government in Europe that'll end wars in Europe. Global government will end global wars. I don't think that's true. Experience shows that the more distinct peoples that have to exist under common government, the more ethnic conflict and hatred there is.

When you talk about global government you are talking about imperial government. You are talking about empire. And it will inevitably be the case that some groups—because they have greater will to power, greater competence in government—will end up ruling over others. A ruling caste will emerge that will be ethnically homogeneous to some extent. That is going to be a source of a great deal of unnecessary conflict and hatred. Right now the EU is a *de facto* German empire. It's what Hitler almost created. Germany calls the shots in the EU, and a lot of countries don't like that. The French don't like this strange situation, because they thought they would be joining the EU to be the ones calling the shots.

It's not a perfect solution, but I think ethnonationalism, by giving each group its homeland, and also by guarding against the encroachment of one country on another, is the way to go. There would be a kind of ethnonationalist world order. There would be another version of the UN. It would be there to help keep people separate, and to keep everything flowing along in the most amicable way possible.

Also, we need institutions to deal with global problems, because there really are global problems. If things like global warming were a reality, it would be a global problem. In that case I would be all for global solutions. One thing that certainly is a global problem is planetary defense. Look up the Shoemaker-Levy comet. It was a comet that hit the surface of Jupiter. If it had hit the Earth, it would have been an extinction event. If the dinosaurs had had a global government, global science, and global defense against comets, then we might not be having this conversation either. There might be lizards debating the virtue of the ethnostate rather than mammals.

I: You know, some would say that that's the case already.

GJ: Ah yes, the lizard people. I find that very amusing. I do think that world peace is a great thing. I think that there will never be global government, because there's always going to be differences between people. The idea that we can live without enemies doesn't really work, because globalists have enemies too. They have enemies like me. Anybody with a bit of ethnic identity and pride is the enemy of the globalist regime, and since ethnic identity and pride will not cease unless there's genocide against all groups by mixing, the globalist utopia is not going to happen.

The globalists tip their hands when they say "The future global citizen will be a homogeneous beige person." Isn't that tantamount to saying that diversity is a problem? Isn't that admitting that diversity is a bad thing? If you are going to have global government, you will need a homogeneous global citizen. Well, that basically is a genocidal project against all the existing peoples of the world.

And instead of declaring your intention to commit racial and cultural genocide against the whole planet in the name of peace, maybe we should just figure out how to make do with the cultural and racial differences that we've got today, so we can actually preserve our differences and live together. I think the route towards that is ethnonationalism for everyone.

I: There are a few ways that you can divide humanity up. You can do it by family if you were satisfied with these super-small microstates. You could also do it geographically, by taste in music, or political affiliation. My question is: Why race in particular? What benefits does an ethnic or racial arrangement provides over other ways of shaping society? Why are racial distinctions more salient than other ones?

GJ: Racial distinctions are more salient because they're more real, and that's the bottom line. There are people who say things like: "I'm a Whovian, and I want to hang out with other *Dr Who* fans. That's my identity." I chuckle at that. That's not a real identity. That's a fake identity that's been foisted upon you by capitalism, by the entertainment business, and you want to embrace this identity because you feel like no one is going to give you any flak for being a Whovian or a Trekkie.

You know you're going to get flak if you say that you are a proud American or a proud white person. For a lot of people, pop culture fandom is just a way of having tribes that are essentially fake, of satisfying a need for identity that's deeply real with fake, politically correct, and non-threatening forms of identity. Non-threatening to whom? To the people who run our societies. They love things like sports: people rooting for their home team. Even if their home team consists of people who aren't from their home, who might be from other continents, they still want to root for their home team.

There's still a desire to have real identity. Real identity is rooted in things that we *don't* choose. So it's rooted in your biology. It's rooted in the culture that you were born into. We don't choose that kind of stuff. It's rooted in what sex you are. It's rooted in class and other things that you don't choose and that affect you before you are ever self-conscious enough to choose them. You learn language before you are self-conscious and rational enough to wonder if it is the language you would have preferred to learn.

We have identities thrust upon us that are real, and race is the one that is the most real because it's literally the warp and woof of our physical being. The same is true of sex. Our second nature is culture, language, those conventions learned before we are self-conscious that are the foundation for any later conscious life and activities. All the "free choices" that we exercise come much later, after we have grown up in a particular culture.

Those two things, biological identity and cultural identity, are real and can't be shrugged off. The only choice we have *vis-à-vis* these things is to be real or fake, to be authentic or inauthentic, to own up to what's been made of us, to be who we are. Or to flee into fake and superficial identities.

People aren't happy in this sort of existence, and that's really the great test. You can't really be happy if you have a superficial and fake existence. It is a matter of being honest and honorable to own up to what you are, to be grateful for what's been given you, to augment it, and to pass it on to the next generation. That's the whole ethical and existential situation that I think we're in. The ethic of liberalism and consumerism and constructing your own identity and so forth, is inauthentic hogwash, and it's no way to run a society.

There are lots of people I know who think that the best way to run a society is like a college team. The college spelling bee team. What do you do? You try to find the best person for every team. Or in a business, what do you do? You try to find the best person for every position. Yes, you will find there is racial and ethnic diversity in such enterprises. There might be certain groups that aren't really good at software, but you can find one or two outliers for your software company. That gives a lot of people the illusion that diversity actually is a great model for society. This is one of the great problems with liberalism and progressivism.

Leo Strauss has an essay called "Progress or Return?" One of the problems he deals with in that essay is the whole foundation of the liberal progressivist interpretation of history, which is science. Look at how science works. It's an enterprise in which it doesn't matter what country you're from as long as you speak the language of mathematics. People contribute to this unfolding, progressive enterprise that goes on into the future and accumulates knowledge and power. The trouble is that's not really a model for society as a whole. The model for society as a whole cannot be a meritocratic enterprise.

A model of society that is closer to the truth is a family group. If you told your son, "Johnny, I'm not going to contribute the money for your college fund, because the neighbor's kid is a standard deviation smarter than you are, and I'll be contributing to his college fund instead" — you'd be a monster! In a society based on ties of blood, you are going to have a bell curve, and you are going to have a few oddball outliers on either end. You're going to have a crazy maiden aunt. You're going to have someone who's a little slower than others. But they are your flesh and blood, and you want to take care of them.

The meritocratic enterprise model, which comes out of business and science and academia, is very tempting, and it sits in the back of the minds of the people who believe that diversity can actually work. It can only work in Silicon Valley, where you are recruiting outliers of various groups in a highly meritocratic process. And face it, they're all subjected to a lot of totalitarian social engineering, as we now know from these Google leaks and lawsuits, because we know it is still an unnatural form of association.

I: With as much of an emphasis as you have been placing on biology so far, I wanted to ask you a hypothetical question. Let's say that your twin society is the pinnacle of social harmony. Couldn't we further divide society up by gender, or even, if we advanced further into the future, reproduce via cloning, and that way you can almost literally have something akin to that twin society that you described. Would it not then be advantageous to also divide society up by gender as well and leave procreation up to the cloning people?

GJ: People would rebel against that because it's more fun to create children the old-fashioned way. You're right, though. Shulamith Firestone, who died a couple of years ago, was a radical feminist who talked about how technology would make it possible to have a society without men. That's true. It can also make it possible to have a society without women. And there might be people, most of them homosexuals, who would be drawn to something like that.

However, it's a strange construct, and it wouldn't really work, because men like women and women like men. Every man today is born of a mother. He often has sisters and female cousins. And yes, there's conflict between the sexes because they are different, but they are also complementary. One of the reasons that people would even consider completely sex-segregated societies is because in modern liberal society there's such confusion about sex, about biologically based sex roles. I don't even use the term gender. Gender is a term from grammar. There's sex, and it's biologically determined. We have a lot of people who are confused about these things, and they're being confused by our culture. There might be oddballs and outliers, biologically speaking, but we're also being fed a whole lot of nonsense about *choosing* genders. How many genders does Google or Facebook have now? 256 genders?

I: I think it's over fifty at this point.

GJ: It's over fifty. It's like going to Baskin Robbins. That's nuts. There's a lot of confusion. I think feminism has created a great deal of unnecessary conflict, as has sexual liberation in general. People don't know how to relate to one another. There are all kinds of risks in relationships, and some people want to flee from that, and some will flee into these technological solutions, like sex dolls, or God forbid, cloning, so you can reproduce without the opposite sex. But I think that's all an indication of how messed up modern society is.

White Nationalism is founded on trying to recover and protect the biological integrity of different racial and sub-racial groups. That necessarily entails a return to biologically-based and tradition-hallowed sexual norms. Once we go back to sanity, we can have a bit of tolerance for the outliers, because we know about the bell curve and so forth. As long as we can uphold the norms and institutions that make it possible for people to do what comes naturally, then I think that the pressures that lead people to those radical solutions will just disappear.

I: I wanted to run an experiment by you because I was thinking of this the other day. Imagine that we're in the year 2050. All the ethnostates have been established, and there's no more work to be done on that. Then one day we read in the newspaper that a brilliant and famous surgeon has been transplanting African brains into the bodies of healthy white newborns. Surgical techniques have become so advanced by this time that there are no scars from him doing this, and by all appearances nothing has actually happened to the white newborns. My question to you is: How would the authorities go about finding all the living victims of his experiments?

GJ: I'm just salivating to say something outrageously racist. Play some funky music or toss them a basketball or something like that. Well, you would find the population of likely victims, and you would give them a battery of tests. You would give them Raven's Matrices and other IQ tests. You'd also give them the Minnesota Multiphasic Personality Inventory. You could give them a whole range of standardized tests, and you would get a pretty good idea who has the African brains, because they would perform, on average, like African brains when they take these tests. The IQs, the levels of sociopathic personality traits, the levels of empathy or lack thereof. There are lots of objective measures by which races can be distinguished.

I: How would you distinguish between them and outliers?

GJ: You would give them a battery of different tests, and therefore the chances of someone being an outlier on all of them would be very, very low. The thing is, I wouldn't be all that worried about it to begin with. Let's say I was a part of the senate of the ethnostate, and I read about this in the newspaper. I'm not going to lose my shit. I'd be glad that the scientist has been stopped. This is Dr. Mengele stuff. What did he do with the white baby brains? We might have a crimewave on our hands if we don't find these people, but even if you find them, what are you going to do? You aren't going to kill them.

I: You could move them to their respective ethnostates.

GJ: But they wouldn't belong there. What I would do is keep an eye on these people, knowing that if they have kids, their kids aren't going to have black genes. It's a problem that would eliminate itself, and it would probably be something I would keep a secret. I'd like to find out who the victims are, and it would be interesting to track them and have their school and criminal records. Follow their life courses. Chances are their life courses will more similar to blacks than whites. It's a problem that eliminates itself biologically with no trace if you leave it alone.

My view of how to get to a white ethnostate is very slow, steady, and patient. If we had the right government by the right principles, time would be on our side. My attitude for people who are of different racial groups who are old and retired is simply to let them live out their lives in retirement. There's a biological solution to that. What I would like to do for the younger ones that are having kids is create incentives to pursue their lives elsewhere. Simply by instituting pro-white incentives and sticking to them you can slowly create a homogeneously white society.

I think that approach is preferable to other more sudden and violent options because I respect human rights. I do believe that all people have rights. Simply meaning there are moral limits on what we can do to others. I believe in animal rights, so I have to believe in human rights, even the rights of other groups that are not compatible with white society. I feel sympathy for them and respect them as living beings. I don't want to harm a hair on their heads, but I do want to create institutions and incentives that over time will slowly create homogeneously white societies.

I want to do it without war, chaos, bloodshed, and catastrophe—the kind of race war scenarios that you find in William Pierce and Harold Covington novels. I think those scenarios are completely unnecessary and frankly just scare the normies. We want to get as many people as possible on board with the idea that ethnonationalism is not only good in theory, but it's also something that can be accomplished with a minimum amount of unpleasantness. In fact, it is actually a way of saving ourselves from a great deal of unpleasantness. The current path that we are on is not going to end well, so the sooner that we get onto the path that respects the rights and the differences of all the peoples of the world, the better.

I: My next question concerns a subject that you have written a bit less about but it really caught my eye, especially when I was reading *New Right vs. Old Right*. In *New Right vs. Old Right* you say that we want to free ourselves of both Jews and Muslims. Let us assume that Judaism is an ethnicity, at least in part. What about Islam though? What if you had a white Muslim. There's nothing impossible about a Dutch Muslim or a Belgian Muslim, etc. Would a white ethnostate prohibit Islam, and equally importantly, how would it do so?

GJ: Islam is a problem because it is an inherently political religion. It promulgates a new regime, a new order of society. It's a law code. As such, therefore, when it exists in a white society or in the proximity of a white society, it is on a collision course. It has to replace that society with its law code and institutions, which were ultimately created in Arabia a long time ago. Therefore, the people who carry this memetic virus, which I consider Islam to be, might be white, but they are like plague rats. They are carrying a memetic plague that will destroy white societies and create societies that are foreign to, and unpleasant for, white people, and therefore they can't be permitted.

Now, what would I do with people who decide to become Muslims? First of all, I would have to make some distinctions here. There are some people who become Muslims because they are interested in philosophy and mysticism and think, "I'll become a Sufi." They're practically not real Muslims, because I don't even think Sufism is real Islam. Sufists were Greco-Roman-Persian pagans who took on Islamic garb because in the Dark Ages it was the only way they could survive. Things like that, I'm okay with, I suppose. Although if you made an exception for Sufis, every Salafist and Wahabi would suddenly declare himself a Sufi. Because deceiving infidels is one of the laws of Islam.

Generally, what I would say to people who believe in Islam is: "You have joined the Islamic community, and we urge you to live according to Islamic law in the Islamic world." I would even give them first-class passage to an Islamic country of their choice. I suspect that some would take me up on that, but most wouldn't.

Again, in present-day society, people convert to Islam for all kinds of reasons. For one, it's just a manifestation of the artificially created alienation and rootlessness of modern liberal society. Just as there are lots of people who are attracted to Asian thought, or Japanese culture. Why are they so attracted to Japanese culture? It is because it is so integral; it's so exotic; it's exotic because it's integral. There's no reason why more integral Western societies that are proud of themselves wouldn't be as satisfying to these weebs as Japan is today. They want to flee a rootless, fake society into things that seem more authentic. Of course, to do so is in itself inauthentic, but that's one of the conditions that we have.

The desire of people to become Muslims would disappear if we had healthier white identities and societies. But if people choose to become Muslims, I would say yes to first-class tickets to the Ummah, all their property sent with them. They would have to realize that they would be killed by their Muslim brothers if they try to become apostates and want to return. It's a one-way trip. The roaches check in, but they don't check out. I would feel sorry for them. But I think honestly that if we drained the swamp of liberal rootlessness and fakery there would be a lot less of that kind of stuff.

I: You consider yourself a Heideggerian, right?

GJ: In many ways, yes.

I: With that thought in mind, what did you think of Dugin's take on Heidegger. I know you're not generally a fan of him.

GJ: I wrote a review of the Dugin book on Heidegger.[1] I didn't think much of it. A lot of it struck me as maximally metaphysical misreadings of Heidegger. It's not an uncommon thing. What he picks out in Heidegger is most consistent with his own messianic Russian nationalism. That's what I find the least appealing about Heidegger, so I'm just not crazy about his book.

I do think that when Dugin talks about *Dasein* and the Fourth Political Theory he is consistent with Heidegger's critique of German National Socialism. Heidegger believed that the prima-

---

[1] Greg Johnson, "Dugin on Heidegger," in *Graduate School with Heidegger* (San Francisco: Counter-Currents, 2020).

ry identity he wanted to defend, namely being German, was not simply reducible to race. Heidegger said that it was mistaking a necessary condition of Germanness, namely being white, for a sufficient one. There was more to being German than being white. When you start treating whiteness as the most important category you start thinking you can just assimilate lots of different people into the German population. The trouble is that this destroys their ethnicities as well as the German one. It would change the Germans as well as the Ukrainians. It would not create the homogeneous beige man but the homogeneous blond man. Heidegger was not too happy with that kind of vision. He wanted the different peoples of Europe to maintain their differences and to figure out a way of differing peacefully with one another, and that I think totally consistent with the New Right as I conceive it, and ethnonationalism as I conceive it.

To some extent, Dugin is right to talk about *Dasein* as opposed to race. For Heidegger, German *Dasein* is white, but it's different from Czech *Dasein* and Danish *Dasein*, even though they're very similar genetically. It's a different culture and different language, and therefore a different world of meaning, a different way of life. That's something worth preserving, which is at the core of identitarian thought.

I: In my reading, I still haven't been able to figure out why Dugin has legs among many on the Alt Right or among White Nationalists. Do you have any theories about why that is the case?

GJ: Gee, no. I've read a couple of his books. I'm not all that impressed. Put it this way, I think if I sat down with him and talked about ideas he would be a very engaging and interesting person, because he reads widely. We can talk about Bataille and Guénon and Evola and Benoist. We've read a lot of the same books. We really might end up being fast friends. He's an admirable person, and I would want more people to traverse his literature. However, I think that too much of what he does is hinged upon apologetics for Russian imperial revanchism, to which I can't be sympathetic.

I: You took the words right out of my mouth with that one, which is why it's so weird to me to see this phenomenon amongst White Nationalists, but maybe it's confined to the few people who I've spoken to about this.

GJ: Right, it's a small thing in the English-speaking world. I don't think he has a lot of followers in the English-speaking world, and I think there are a lot of people who are curious about him. I admire people who are curious about him, and I hope that his books continue to be read. It's still infinitely superior to the shelves groaning with books by Foucault and Derrida. I wish him well, but I think that at his heart he is opposed to ethnonationalism. He is for Russian imperialism, and I am not for that. I sympathize with the Estonians and Latvians and Lithuanians. I think that Russia itself would be better off if it gave up this deep-seated mentality that is so similar to the mentality of Americans. It is a messianic nationalism, a sense of messianic destiny.

The trouble with that sort of nationalism is that it is an engine of miscegenation and erasure of identity. At *Counter-Currents*, check out Jarosław Ostrogniew's four-part review of Alexiey Shiropayev's *Prison of the Nation* about how the Russian imperialist machine has been at war with the Russian nation from the very beginning.

This was true of Rome and Byzantium. Rome became a machine that liquidated the founding population of Rome and kept bringing in new peoples and liquidating them, creating a kind of imperial man, and it did so at the expense of the distinct groups who founded it. Byzantium did the same thing. By the sixth century or so there were no more Romans in Byzantium. They had been replaced with people from all over the empire. It had destroyed its own founding stock.

The Third Rome did the same thing. The first nonwhite to rule Russia was Boris Godunov, who was mostly Tatar in his ancestry, and this was at the beginning of the seventeenth century. The machine treated anyone who swore allegiance to the Tsar, spoke Russian, and followed the Orthodox church as a Russian. This included many powerful Tatars, who found themselves under Muscovite rule when the Golden Horde collapsed after the great standoff with Ivan III. These Tatars could become Russians simply by changing their religious and political allegiances. And they immediately had higher status than the vast majority of ethnic Russians, who were little more than slaves.

Muscovy was a machine that melded together Byzantium and Mongol/Oriental Despotism, and it's been profoundly destructive of the ethnic genetic interests of anyone who has fallen into its clutches. Which is not to say that the Nazi idea that all Russians are miscegenated with Mongols is entirely true. But it's partly true. And it is true that the Russian imperial mentality has been very destructive of the ethnic differences of the various peoples in that empire.

Today, under Putin, Moscow has a giant mosque. He thinks that having all these Muslims in the Caucasus under his control makes Moscow more powerful. If you are critical of Muslims in Russia you are frowned upon. To keep the powerful Russian machine going, Putin is willing to stamp down on the ethnocentrism of the native Russian population. That's not a good system. It is similar to the system we have in America today. We are ruled by people who are opposed to the ethnic genetic interests of the founding stock of the country. Eventually we got a nonwhite ruler, Obama, but this came a long time later than what happened in Russia with Boris Godunov.

I: You've voiced a partiality to certain forms of pluralism, religious pluralism being one of them. In the very introduction to *New Right vs. Old Right* you go so far as to say that the North American New Right is an inherently pluralistic movement. When I read that, the philosopher in me started scratching his head. Why is pluralism *vis-à-vis* religion or certain approaches to Right-wing politics desirable whilst pluralism *vis-à-vis* race or culture is undesirable? What is the philosophically relevant factor that makes the question of race categorically different to others?

GJ: What I mean by pluralism is that there are many different systems of axioms and starting points that lead people to conclude that ethnonationalism is a good thing. Therefore, we have people in our midst who are scientific materialists, and we have people who are into Traditionalism and things like that. We have people with different religious outlooks: Christians, atheists, agnostics, mystics. I know lots of people who are into Hinduism, Taoism, and European paganism. There is an inherent pluralism in religious thought also, that I think is consistent with white ethnonationalism. There are some religions that aren't consistent with that. I want to respect the range of pluralism that still leads to ethnonationalist conclusions.

I also have my own views on these matters, and in the next few years I am going to set out my own "system." As Blake said, if you don't create your own system you become a slave to another man's. I have a system of ideas that I have worked out over time studying philosophy, and I want to put it out there. People can take it or leave it.

I: That's fascinating. When do you think we can expect that?

GJ: In 2018, I'm putting out the *White Nationalist Manifesto*. Also I'm working on a piece called "A Philosophical Agenda," which is a system program like those you might find in German Idealism. After that I'm going to work on a couple of books. One is going to be called *Identity Politics*, and it's going to lay out the metaphysical, epistemological, and anthropological foundations of identity politics.

I am also going to do a book outlining the political philosophy of the ethnostate. There will be a lot of different regimes in ethnostates. If you look at the history of Europe, there have been radically different forms of government. But there are certain basic political principles that I want to defend. I want to put my cards on the table. If my views can be improved upon, I'd like to see them improved upon.

One of the reasons I think the movement hasn't really gelled into creating institutions as impressive as those of say, the libertarian movement, is that the libertarians have "doctrines." They put out big books, the big canonical works of Austrian economics or Objectivism, which lay out a "system" of ideas. Not that I think they hang together very well as systems of ideas.

I: Right!

GJ: But the very fact that libertarianism puts itself forward as a system of ideas that will allow you to lead a certain kind of life, leads a lot of people to glom onto it, and when they do so, they create institutions that propagate that view. I think that we really need people to step forward and say, "Here's a system," a doctrine. Read it, tell me what you think of it, and if you want to sign off on this, we can start figuring out ways of propagating it more effectively. At that point, the movement is still going to be pluralistic, but I will be playing a stronger role, taking my own side, advancing my own particular views.

Of course, I'm still going to be publishing people who disagree with me, because I think that's part of creating an exciting intellectual movement. One needs to create platforms with intellectual diversity. Not everyone has to be marching in lockstep in the same direction. A lot of taking part in intellectual movements is more like twirling around on the dance floor together for fun. People aren't all moving in the same direction. But it's fun, and people want to join the dance.

I want this movement to be fun and stimulating. I want this to be what the Left used to be, generations ago now, something exciting and stimulating. It's not that way anymore. It's a bunch of po-faced, dour, blue-haired crazies. It is no fun if you are afraid to disagree with these people, afraid to think. I want the New Right in America, first and foremost, to be intellectually exciting. Second, I want to be putting my views out there and defending them as mine. Then we will see if things might gel around that to create political and historical change.

I: This is what I would like to consider my fun question. It's fun for me, and it's been fun for everyone else I've given it to. If you could force every Leftist to read just five books and reckon with the arguments therein, which five would you choose?

GJ: That's a really good question. Someday, I hope that I can list five books of my own for this. First, would be Jared Taylor's *White Identity*; the second would be Phillipe Rushton's *Race, Evolution and Behavior*; the third would be one of Richard Lynn's books like *IQ and Global Inequality*, where he talks about just the effects of IQ differences on a whole host of social outcomes.

A fourth book definitely would be Kevin MacDonald's *Culture of Critique*. Maybe a book that we could stick in there before people read *The Culture of Critique* is Israel Shahak's book *Jewish History, Jewish Religion*, which is a very short book written by a Jewish dissident; it's something you can read in a single sitting. It would really prime people for Kevin Macdonald's book. I'm guessing that these would be somewhat intellectual Leftists, so if they were anything like me in their exposure to certain Jewish intellectual movements, they are going to have some questions and puzzles that they have set aside for future reflection that will be very powerfully solved by reading someone like Kevin MacDonald.

Those books would be quite mind-blowing, and if people actually grappled with those I think a lot of them would have to start changing their political paradigm. The next book I would have them read would be my *White Nationalist Manifesto*. That would be number six.

I: You can keep going you know. You don't have to limit yourself to five.

GJ: I know, but five is good. The chances of people reading ten books as opposed to five are much lower.

I: That's all I've got, Greg. Do you have anything you'd like to add?

GJ: No, this has been pleasant and enjoyable. Let's leave it at this for now, and we could continue this conversation in the future.

I: Yes, I'd be happy to. I've certainly enjoyed it.

Counter-Currents, July 2, 2019

STRAIGHT BUT NOT NARROW NATIONALISM

INTERVIEW WITH MAUREEN O'CONNOR*

MAUREEN O'CONNOR: Do you consider yourself a White Nationalist?

GREG JOHNSON: Yes. White Nationalism is a species of ethnonationalism, which is the view that the best political order is to create sovereign racially and ethnically homogeneous homelands for all peoples that aspire to autonomy.

MO: What role do gay, bisexual, or queer people have in your movement?

GJ: There have always been such people in our movement at all levels, from simple supporters and donors to organizers and activists. Martin Webster, for instance, was one of the central organizers and activists in the UK for decades. Although we have not done any empirical studies yet, based on more than sixteen years of involvement in White Nationalism, I would say that our movement is far less gay than the Republicans.

MO: What about transgender people? How do you feel about trans issues, like laws on bathroom use?

GJ: I know of three transgender people in our movement. They are decent men who now think they are women. I believe that a compassionate society should help people who are suffering, but I also think that society should say "no" to gender

---

* Maureen O'Connor at *New York Magazine* sent me some questions by email in April of 2017. It was a background interview for an article focusing mostly on Jack Donovan. These are my answers. Only a few of my words were used in her article, "Philosophical Fascists of the Gay Alt-Right," *New York Magazine*, April 30, 2017.

switching. People's sex is determined by their chromosomes. "Gender" is a term from grammar. It has no place in the discussion of sexuality. Sex is a biological category, not a social construct. I believe that hormones and surgery to turn someone into a simulacrum of the opposite sex is not a cure or solution to the underlying discontent that motivates it. I would ban it altogether. Transsexuals admit they suffer from a mental illness. But in this case, instead of trying to cure them of their delusions, society is supposed to humor them and aid and abet irreversible self-mutilation. In the end, the risk of suicide is higher — an outcome that would disqualify a "treatment" for any other mental illness. The fact that transgenderism has become a liberal crusade and is now being extended to children is monstrous and really proof that liberalism passed from ideology into the realm of madness.

MO: What role does religion play in your movement, and what role do you think it should play?

GJ: Our movement is about race and ethnicity. That is what unifies us. Religion only divides us. To the extent that our movement functions at all, it is by persuading people to make religion a secondary issue. Which means that a certain amount of religious pluralism and tolerance is baked into our movement and into the society that we will create in the future.

MO: What role does sex have in your vision for society?

GJ: In today's sexually liberated society, people talk more about sex, think more about sex, and look at more images of sex than ever before. But on average they have less sex and probably also enjoy it less than past generations. They form families later, have more brittle relationships and marriages, and have fewer children than in the past as well. Venereal diseases and sexual assaults are up, though. In the sexual realm, as in the culture as a whole, we are miserable because we are free. People have too many options, so they never commit, so they experience the pleasures of marriage and family life late or not at all.

In the society I envision, we would restore some of the restraints on sex. Not because it is dirty, but because it is sacred. Feminism, pickup artists, *Cosmo*, pornography, and I suppose this very discussion would not exist. But there would be statues of gorgeous naked nymphs and athletes in every public square. There would be stigmas on promiscuity and extramarital sex. Marriage bonds would be stronger. Divorce would be rare and difficult. There would be eugenic incentives to encourage people who are intelligent and socially and ecologically responsible to have larger families and people who are stupid and don't care about the world to have smaller families (precisely the opposite of what we have now).

The consequence of these policies would be that more people would have more access to better quality sex within the context of long-term relationships. Better people would have better children. And the human race would be nudged back on the upward evolutionary path.

MO: Your "gay panic" article discusses female participation, and gay male participation, in the Alt Right.[1] Do you know any gay or queer women in the Alt Right?

GJ: There are a few, although I don't know them personally. I do know a couple of ex-lesbians who now have husbands and children.

MO: You say White Nationalism should be "straight but narrow." What does that look like, in practice? How can you tell if a movement—or person—is "straight but narrow"?

GJ: I said that White Nationalism should be straight but *not* narrow. Meaning that we should uphold heterosexuality as the norm and yet not get bent out of shape about the fact that some people inevitably do not fit the norm.

Counter-Currents, April 30, 2017

---

[1] Greg Johnson, "Gay Panic on the Alt Right," *In Defense of Prejudice* (San Francisco: Counter-Currents, 2017).

What's Wrong with Modernity?

Interview with
Liz Bruenig*

Liz Bruenig: Do you consider yourself Alt Right or neoreactionary or something along those lines? (Also, how would you like to be introduced — as an editor, writer, etc.?)

Greg Johnson: I am a writer, editor, and publisher. I call myself a White Nationalist, because my goal is the creation of sovereign homelands for all European peoples who aspire to autonomy. In terms of my strategy for political change, I describe myself as a New Rightist, meaning that I focus on the metapolitical conditions of political change, including transforming people's ideas and values and creating new forms of community. I would describe myself as an Alt Rightist insofar as that is a vague term that encompasses a wide rage of alternatives to mainstream conservatism, including White Nationalism and the New Right. I do not describe myself as a neo-reactionary, because although that particular movement parallels my ideas in some respects (while diverging in others), it had no influence on my thinking and holds itself aloof from White Nationalism.

LB: What's the matter with modernity?

GJ: That's a big question.

A major problem with modernity is the bedrock assumption of modern science and technology that the world is in principle transparent to reason and available for technological manipulation, which casts man as the master and possessor of nature. This attitude gives rise to the glib hubris behind most of the errors of progressive social policy, particularly egalitarian so-

---

* Liz Bruenig sent me some questions by email in 2017. These are my answers, published here for the first time.

cial engineering schemes.

A related problem is the idea of the social construction of race and gender. Social constructivism is really just a metaphysical postulate of egalitarian social engineering schemes, which assume that man is "perfectible" and malleable. Race and sex, however, are biological realities that cannot be altered by merely political means. (Political policy can change race only by imposing eugenic or dysgenic breeding patterns.) Progressives, of course, are happy to appeal to nature when they want to excuse something (homosexuality, obesity). But anything they want to change—such as racial and sexual inequality—is declared a social construct.

Another problem with modernity is its pervasive individualism and subjectivism in the realm of ethics and politics. The idea of the individual emancipated from unchosen identities and obligations who is able to posit his own values destroys the idea of objective goods to which the will must submit and the idea that our identity derives from our lineage, culture, and social station, none of which we choose. Individualism basically licenses people to identify themselves with a set of "given preferences" (without being too critical about just how those preferences are formed) and then to seek out only those social interactions that satisfy those preferences.

This ethos undermines all institutions that seek to elevate and change people's preferences: marriage, family life, education, religion, civic participation, etc. All of these institutions are being hollowed out and replaced by essentially market transactions that service given preferences rather than challenge us to embrace better, deeper, and nobler ones. The result: immature and unactualized individuals and dysfunctional institutions.

Another problem with modern individualism is the denial that the common good of a society exists, or is knowable, or that it needs to be promoted by the state.

LB: Can you pinpoint a moment in history where things went off the rails for the West? What precipitated things degenerating to the point we're at now?

GJ: Everything bad about modernity is rooted in Christian theology, which became secularized in the early modern era, giving rise to nominalism in metaphysics and epistemology (the mutability of reality and the conventional nature of differences between the races and sexes) and egalitarian individualism in ethics and politics.

Everything about our society that is decent and not dysfunctional is basically rooted in pre-modern institutions, practices, and traditions that modernity is slowly destroying. Modernity is living off the capital of premodern civilization, and when that capital is exhausted, the modern world will collapse. Modernity in itself has no substance. It is a parasitic phenomenon.

LB: What writers are most important to you?

GJ: The writers who most shaped my thinking are Plato, Aristotle, Vico, Rousseau, Kant, Hegel, Nietzsche, and Heidegger. A second tier of thinkers who strongly influenced my understanding and appreciation of the first tier include Carl Schmitt, Leo Strauss, Alexandre Kojève, René Guénon, Julius Evola, Savitri Devi, Alain de Benoist, and Guillaume Faye. Kevin MacDonald's work on Jewish intellectual movements, especially *The Culture of Critique*, has been a strong influence.

My favorite poets are W. B. Yeats and Robinson Jeffers. My favorite essayists and critics are Ezra Pound, D. H. Lawrence, and Camille Paglia. H. P. Lovecraft and Flannery O'Connor are my favorite fiction writers.

LB: What role does history play in Alt-Right reasoning? Is there an ideal polity in history that you look to for inspiration?

GJ: For me, the primary value of history is that you can prove that something is possible if you can show that it was actual. I don't think any historical regime is ideal, though some were better than others. Every functional European society seems to arrive at a mixed constitution, with monarchical, aristocratic, and democratic elements, which is for me the ideal form of government. Every functioning society also arrives at something resembling fascism—in a generic, small-f sense of the term—if it seeks to harmonize private interests with the common good, harmonize labor and capital, impart patriotism and civic mindedness, inculcate virtues, and so forth. Ultimately, though, a government's goodness does not depend on concrete institutions or written constitutions, but on the quality and character of the people. One of the great follies of modernity is thinking we can have a good society without good men.

LB: What period of artwork/film/literature etc. speaks to you?

GJ: Beauty speaks to me. Sublimity speaks to me. Vitality speaks to me. I can forgive a lot that is florid and grotesque if it is vital. Good taste and good craftsmanship speak to me.

I love Ancient Egyptian, Assyrian, Persian, Greek, and Roman art.

In architecture, Roman, Gothic, Renaissance, Baroque, Jugendstil, Art Deco, and Wright.

In music, Bach, Handel, Mozart, Beethoven, Wagner, Brahms, Puccini, Elgar, and Richard Strauss.

My very favorite painters are Dürer, Van Dyck, Jacques-Louis David, Caspar David Friedrich, Franz von Stuck, and Dalí (especially his huge, late works). I prefer the northern Renaissance to the Italian. I love minor Dutch paintings from the seventeenth and eighteenth centuries. In the nineteenth century, generally I love everything that the Impressionists hated. In the twentieth century, I love Wyndham Lewis' paintings, as well as the Italian Futurists, Grant Wood, Edward Hopper, and Thomas Hart Benton.

My favorite director is David Lynch.

Aesthetically, I believe that the peak of white civilization was the late nineteenth century to the beginning of the First World War.

LB: How did you come to this way of thinking? What was your life like before? What's it like now?

GJ: I came to my present positions by going through life with my eyes open. I would analyze what people say but also observe what they do. A lot of the discrepancies are caused not just by individual weakness and selfishness but by ethnic political agendas. I came to realize that individualism crippled my psychological development and blinded me to the central importance of race and ethnic identity for politics. But now I see. And that changed everything.

INDEX

Numbers in bold refer to a whole chapter or section devoted to a particular topic.

9/11, 41

A
academia, 3, 6–7, 193
aesthetics, 17, 176, 179, 211
agency, 52, 97
alienation, 8–9, 21, 92, 131, 141, 187, 198
American Renaissance, 131
ancestors & ancestry, 61–62, 65–67, 135–36, 139, 200
anthropology, 11, 202
anti-colonialism, 52, 116
Anti-Defamation League, 41
antisemitism, 41–42
Archeofuturism, 45
aristocracy, 23–24, 30, 45
Aristotle, 23, 82, 126, 170, 175, 185
Artaxerxes II, 33
Asians, 43, 65, 103, 108, 119, 142, 198
assimilation, 13, 18, 40, 137–38, 140–41, 155, 199
Atlas Shrugged, 13, 133
atomization, 23
Australia, 2, 22, 30, 41, 47
Austrian economics, 202

B
Bach, Johann Sebastian, 211
bad faith, 168

Balkans, 32
Bataille, Georges, 199
beauty, 5, 162, 164–66, 168, 180, 211
Beethoven, Ludwig van, 211
bell curve distribution, 40, 130, 149, 193, 194
Benoist, Alain de, 75, 199, 210
Benton, Thomas Hart, 211
Berlin Wall, the, 118–19
Black Lives Matter, 16
blacks, 15, 22, 63, 65, 71, 100, 102, 103, 108–109, 115, 116, 138–39, 145, 149–50, 151–52, 195–96
Blake, William, 82, 202
Boas, Franz, 10
Bolshevism, 37
Bonaparte, Napoleon, 35
borders, 14, 34, 39, 47, 49, 59–60, 66, 79, 114, 118–19, 125, 137, 142–43, 162
bourgeois ethics, 3, 27, 30, 45
Bowden, Jonathan, 75, 93
Brahms, Johannes, 211
Brexit, 69
Brimelow, Peter, 37
British National Party, 79
Bruenig, Liz, **208–12**
Bush, George H. W., 32
Bush, George W., 41

Byzantium, 5, 200–201

C
Canada, 2, 54, 58, 111, 137, 162
capitalism, 23–24, 27, 29, 41, 46–47, 51, 76, 80, 87, 210, 211
Catholicism, 25, 40, 44
Charlotte, 145
Charlottesville, 157
Christianity, 16–18, 25, 39, 40, 87, 88–89, 137, 202, 210
civic nationalism, 17, 29, 70, 105
classical liberalism, 12, 127
classical music & musicians, 165, 211
Clinton, Hillary, 37
codependency, 19–20
Cold-Blooded Kindness, 19
common good, the, 24–25, 36, 45, 63, 125–27, 151–53, 209, 211
communism, 5, 32, 41, 71, 76, 77, 80, 125, 158
consumerism, 2, 27, 192
coolness, 93, 95, 105–106, 110, 163, 179
Cooper, Darryl, **1–47**
Counter-Currents, 1, 3, 28, 48, 70, 71, 73, 82, 86, 95, 96, 113, 119, 123, 133, 134, 136, 147, 158, 160, 200
Covington, Harold, 196
creationism, 17–18, 121
cultural Marxism, 16, 122

culture, 4, 9, 10, 11, 22, 27, 29, 31, 59, 71, 76, 77, 81, 115, 122, 132, 134–38, 151, 153, 157, 177, 178, 182, 185, 186, 188, 191, 192, 194, 198, 199, 201, 206, 209
Culture of Critique, 204, 210
Cyrus, 33
Czechs, 32, 182, 199

D
Dalí, Salvador, 211
Darius, 33
Darwinism, 44
Dasein, 198–99
David, Jacques-Louis, 211
deaths of despair, 61
Decline of the West (podcast), **1–47**
Decline of the West (Spengler), 9
Deen, Paula, 111
Defamation, 41
democracy, 23–24, 44, 45, 77, 82, 179, 210
Democrats, 21–22, 37
demographic replacement, 14, 49; *see also* racial replacement
demographics, 2, 12–15, 43, 48–49, 58, 63, 69, 70, 156
Derrida, Jacques, 200
Detroit, 145
discipline, 169
diversity, 21, 23, 49–50, 56–57, 64, 85, 88, 111, 149, 154, 163, 185, 187–88, 190,

192–93, 203
divorce, 117, 207
Donovan, Jack, 160, 174
drugs, 38
Dugin, Aleksandr, 198–99
Dune (novel), 45
Dürer, Albrecht, 211
dysgenics, 184, 209

E

economy, the, 2, 7, 14, 25–26, 46–47, 51, 63, 76, 114, 125–26, 129, 133, 202
education, 6, 7, 16, 18, 39, 54, 82, 83–84, 94, 120–26, 129, 130, 132, 138, 153, 170, 173
egalitarianism, 11, 17, 75, 167–68, 180, 184, 208–210
egotism, 20, 28
Egypt, ancient, 5, 211
Elgar, Edward, 211
elitism, 75, 81–83, 168–70, 179
Enlightenment, the, 10, 74,
environmentalism, 87–88, 143
Epicureanism, 10
Estonia, 30, 200
ethnic cleansing, 60, 119
ethnocentrism, 40, 52, 54–55, 57, 114, 146–48, 155–56, 201
ethnonationalism, 29, 34, 58, 140, 188, 190, 196, 199–202
eugenics, 44, 149, 184, 207, 209

Europe, 2, 9, 14, 18, 22, 44, 45, 49, 50, 51, 54, 57, 58, 62, 63, 65, 66, 67, 71, 86, 99, 105, 106, 114, 138, 140–45, 162, 163, 177, 178, 180, 189, 199, 202, 208; Jews in Europe, 35–36, 38–40; Pan-Europeanism 28–34
Evola, Julius, 10, 199, 210
evolution, 10, 17, 121, 181–84, 188, 207

F

factionalism, 24–25, 126
fairness, 13, 15, 44, 53, 57–58, 69, 141
faith, 18
fake hate crimes, 42
Farrow, Mia, 102
fascism, 38, 47, 79–80, 178, 210
Faustian man, 187
Faye, Guillaume, 45, 210
fear, 22, 26, 39, 104, 175
feminism, 6, 81, 88, 96–99, 123, 155, 193, 194, 206
Firestone, Shulamith, 193
Foucault, Michael, 12, 200
Francis, Sam, 147
Friedrich, Caspar David, 211
free trade, 125
free will, 186, 192
Freud, Sigmund, 27–28

G

game theory, 13, 17, 36,
gay liberation, 38

gay panic, 207
Generation Z, 69
genetic determinism, 103, 186
Genetic Similarity Theory, 22, 101, 154, 183–84, 186–88
genocide, 58–60, 76, 81, 86, 89, 154–55, 190
German Idealism, 202
Gladwell, Malcolm, 19
global warming, 142, 190
globalism, 13, 25, 46–47, 50–51, 80, 125, 133, 189–90
God, 6, 18, 175, 185
Godunov, Boris, 200–201
Golden Dawn, 115
Golden Horde, the, 200
Gramsci, Antonio, 76
Griffin, Nick, 79
Guénon, Réne, 199, 210
guilt, 52, 54–55, 57, 61, 64, 101, 107, 109, 114, 135–36

H

Haidt, Jonathan, 21
Handel, George Frideric, 211
hatred, 4, 15, 40, 64, 69, 109, 133, 151, 169, 189
Hegel, G. W. F., 27, 210
hegemony, 76–77, 80, 123–24
Heidegger, Martin, 198–99, 210
Herbert, Frank, 45
Herzl, Theodor, 42
Heyerdahl, Thor, 4–5
hoarding, 19–20

Hobbes, Thomas, 27, 132
Holmes, Steven, 10
Holocaust, 39, 40, 58, 120
homeschooling, 124
homosexuality & homosexuals, 100, 193, 209
honor, 11, 27–28, 160, 173–74, 192
Hopper, Edward, 211
human biodiversity, 18
Hume, David, 27
hypocrisy, 146–49, 154

I

identity, 1, 17, 23, 30–31, 42, 70, 74, 78, 84, 148, 152, 178, 179, 187, 188, 190–91, 198, 200, 209, 212
identity politics, 53, 202
immigration, 13–14, 20, 39, 42–43, 44, 50, 55, 56, 59–60, 88, 114, 141, 144, 150
imperialism, 28, 31–34, 52, 76, 80, 140, 189, 199–201
Imperium (book), 28
imperium (idea), 32, 34
individualism, 13, 17, 36, 54–55, 57, 121, 126–32, 151–53, 209, 212
inequality, 75, 172, 176
IQ & Global Inequality, 203
Islam, 49, 58, 88, 197–98; *see also* Muslims
Italian Futurism, 211

J

J. M., **134–59**

Japan & Japanese, 16, 42, 117, 145, 161, 198
Jeffers, Robinson, 210
Jesus, 16, 33
Jewish History, Jewish Religion, 204
Jewish question, the, 34–35, 67, 80
Jews, 16, 34–42, 67, 80–81, 83, 87–89, 108, 109, 113–16, 123, 148, 197, 204, 210
John Birch Society, 37
Jolie, Angelina, 102
justice, 77–79, 82

K
King's Peace, 33
Kojève, Alexandre, 210

L
La Rochefoucauld, François VI, Duc de, 146
labor movement, the, 45
LARPing, 31, 43–44
Latin America, 49
Latvia, 32, 200
Lawrence, D. H., 210
Leftism, 15–17, 36–38, 50–52, 64, 69, 75–78, 80, 88, 90, 91, 110, 120–23, 135, 145–47, 151, 156, 166–68, 179, 203–204
lesbians, 87, 207
liberals & liberalism, 10, 12, 17–18, 20–22, 25–27, 38, 45, 54, 64, 68, 73, 75, 80, 81, 102, 122, 124–25, 127, 130–31, 133, 145–46, 151, 153–54, 168, 192, 194, 198, 206; liberal democracy, 23, 24, 45, 77; liberal society, 17, 125, 151, 194, 198
liberty, 23, 25–26, 32
Lithuania, 200
Locke, John, 27, 132
Lokteff, Lana, **73–95**
Lovecraft, H. P., 210
Lynch, David, 211
Lynn, Richard, 150, 203

M
MacDonald, Hugh, **96–113, 160–180**
MacDonald, Kevin, 114, 146, 204, 210
"magic dirt," 18
Mann, A. Wyatt, 101
Manosphere, 116
marriage, 38, 65, 206–207, 209
Marx, Karl, 37
Marxism, 15, 17, 76, 99, 106, 117, 122, 124
mass transportation, 144
materialism, 9, 19, 30, 186, 201
McCarthy, Kevin, 28
McCarthy, Tara, **48–72**
media, the, 54, 107, 118, 123–26
mental health, 61
mental illness, 206
metaphysics, 9–10, 11, 25, 181, 182, 185, 186, 198, 202, 210

metapolitics, 1, 84–86, 116, 208
millennials, 69
Millennial Woes, **113–33**
miscegenation, 2, 64–66, 114, 118, 151, 155, 200–201
monarchy, 23–24, 210
Mozart, Wolfgang Amadeus, 211
multiculturalism, 2, 12, 14, 18, 21, 23, 38–39, 50, 52–54, 57, 58, 64, 69, 77, 114, 119, 124, 141, 142, 143, 145, 147, 155, 158, 163, 178
Murros, Kai, 93
Muslims, 22–23, 27, 34, 38–39, 41, 49, 56, 58, 77, 140, 151–52, 197–98, 201; *see also* Islam

N

narcissism, 28, 171–73
National Action, 115
National Geographic, 11
National Review, 28, 73
National Socialism, 9, 79–80, 198
nation-state, the, 48–49
NATO, 34, 144
NAXALT, 130, 152
neoconservatism, 37, 73
neoreaction, 208
nepotism, 17, 53
New Right, 75–77, 81, 95, 199, 208; European, 75; North American, 1, 75, 201, 203

New Right vs. Old Right, 75, 91, 123, 197, 201
New York Magazine, 205
Nietzsche, Friedrich, 10, 210
nihilism, 61, 156–57
NoMoreDogma, 134
normies, 22, 134, 159, 196
North American New Right, 1, 73

O

Oakley, Barbara, 19
obesity, 209
occult warfare, 84
Occupy movement, the, 8
Old Right, 75–77
O'Connor, Flannery, 210
O'Connor, Maureen, **205–207**
Ostrogniew, Jarosław, 200

P

Paglia, Camille, 210
pathological altruism, 19–20
peace, 20, 25–27, 32–34, 37, 48–49, 50, 55, 74, 78, 156, 188–90, 199
Persian Empire, 33, 197, 211
Pierce, William Luther, 196
Pinker, Steven, 28
Plantation economics, 45, 47, 51, 133
Plato, 11, 27, 210
pluralism, 81, 123, 201–203, 206
Polignano, Michael, 1
political correctness, 6–7, 71, 78, 191

Politics (Aristotle), 23, 126
populism, 82–83, 89, 158, 168, 179
pornography, 38, 157, 206
Pound, Ezra, 210
pretentiousness, 160, 165–68, 170, 178, 180
pride, 27, 61, 135–36, 161, 163, 190
private property, 23–25
progressivism, 21, 45, 192, 208–209
Progressive Movement, the, 44–45
propaganda, 43, 64, 84, 102, 104, 121, 122, 146, 163
protectionism, 25
Protestantism, 25, 39
Protestant Reformation, the, 25
psychology, 4, 11, 20, 21, 27, 61–62, 103, 104, 110, 116, 146, 154, 156, 171–73, 183, 184, 212
Puccini, Giacomo, 211
Putnam, Robert, 9, 21

R
race, 9–13, 16, 22, 34, 53–55, 77–80, 84, 87–88, 94, 128–29, 146–47, 150, 181–86, 190–91, 195, 199, 209, 210; *see also* race realism, race replacement, racism
Race, Evolution & Behavior, 183
race realism, 12–13, 34
race replacement, 88, 114; *see also* demographic replacement
racism, **96–113**
Rand, Ayn, 133
reactionism, 10, 44, 179, 208
Reality Calls, 48
rebelliousness, 105, 178
Red Ice Radio, 95
Republic (Plato), 27
republicanism, 23, 46
Republicans, 13, 15, 17, 21, 37, 205
Robb, John, 13
Rome, 5, 49, 197, 200, 211
Romeo & Juliet, 117, 151, 153
Romney, Mitt, 17
Rousseau, Jean-Jacques, 172, 210
Rushton, J. Phillipe, 183, 203
Russia, 32, 34, 198–201
Russian Orthodox Church, 200

S
Sargon of Akkad, **113–33**
Savitri Devi, 210
Schmitt, Carl, 24, 210
scientific materialism, 186, 210; *see also* materialism
Second World War, 58–59, 69, 76
secret societies, 17
self-expression, 177–78
self-improvement, 170, 173
selfishness, 2, 131, 156, 211
sex, 45, 94, 131, 191, 194, 206, 209, 210
sexual assault, 206

sexual liberation, 194, 206
sexuality, 38, 98, 99, 129, 147, 206–207
Shahak, Israel, 42, 204
shaming, 61, 96–99, 135
Shamir, Yoav, 41
Sharansky, Natan, 41
Shelbyville, 157
Shiropayev, Alexiey, 200
Shklar, Judith, 26
skeptic community, 113
skepticism, 131–32
slurs, 99–100, 102, 104–105, 108–109
snobbery, 84, 160, 167–68, 180
Sobran, Joseph, 37
social constructivism, 11–12, 99, 184, 209
social credit, 47
social media, 71, 115, 157
Southern Poverty Law Center, 115
sovereignty, 2, 24–25, 34–35, 43, 48, 78–79, 138, 143, 205, 208
Spencer, Richard, 28, 31–32, 185
Spengler, Oswald, 9–10
Spinoza, Baruch, 132
Stewart, Jon, 15
stigma, 98–99, 106–110, 207
Strauss, Leo, 192, 210
Strauss, Richard, 211
Stuck, Franz von, 211
subjectivism, 209
Sufism, 197
suicide, 61, 87, 88, 125, 206

T

taboos, 4, 43
tabula rasa, 146
taste, 83, 165–66, 168, 170–71, 179, 186–87, 191, 211
Tatars, 200–201
Taylor, Jared, 203
Taylor, Robert 92–93
technology, 5, 27, 45–47, 96, 99, 142, 193–94, 208
Thiel, Peter, 46
Third Reich, 10
thumos, 28
totalitarianism, 76–77, 80, 116, 119, 193
Traditionalism, 202
transgenderism, 205–206
tripartition of the soul, 11, 27
Trotskyism, 37
Trump, Donald, 16–17, 21, 25, 28, 37, 45, 69, 71
twins, 103, 186–87, 193

U

United Kingdom, the, 55–56, 205
United Nations, the, 58, 137, 144, 189
United States, the, 2, 9, 22, 28–30, 32, 34, 35, 38–39, 47, 49, 51, 54, 56–57, 59–61, 63, 78, 90, 117, 119, 124, 137, 138, 143, 144–45

V

van Dyck, Anthony 211
vanity, 160–66, 171–73, 175, 177–80

Vico, Giambattista, 10, 210
virtue, 120–21, 146, 160, 170–72, 179, 187, 190, 211
Vox Day, 31

W
Wagner, Richard, 211
Walker, Michael, 131
Webster, Martin, 205
white dispossession, 86–87, 89
white flight, 56
white guilt; *see* guilt
White Identity (Jared Taylor), 203
white nationalism, 8, 13, 16, 20–21, 29, 34, 42, 43, 48, 58, 69–70, 72, 79, 81, 84, 88, 91–92, 94, 103, 105, 108–109, 113–14, 122, 131, 137, 185–86, 194, 200, 202, 205, 207, 208
White Nationalist Manifesto, 202, 204

white man's burden, 52
white supremacism, 70–71, 106, 137–40, 142, 143
Wise, Tim, 148
Wittelsbach family and palace, 61–62
Wood, Grant, 211
women, 6, 16, 38, 74, 88, 94, 97–99, 103, 105, 123, 129–31, 152, 164, 171, 177, 193, 205, 207
women's lib, 38

X
Xerxes, 33

Y
Yeats, W. B., 210
Yockey, Francis Parker, 28
Yugoslavia, 32

Z
Zionism, 4, 37–38, 42

About the Author

GREG JOHNSON, Ph.D. is Editor-in-Chief of Counter-Currents Publishing Ltd. and the *Counter-Currents* webzine (http://www.counter-currents.com/).

He is the author of *Confessions of a Reluctant Hater* (San Francisco: Counter-Currents, 2010; expanded edition, 2016), *Trevor Lynch's White Nationalist Guide to the Movies* (Counter-Currents, 2012), *New Right vs. Old Right* (Counter-Currents, 2013), *Son of Trevor Lynch's White Nationalist Guide to the Movies* (Counter-Currents, 2015), *Truth, Justice, & a Nice White Country* (Counter-Currents, 2015), *In Defense of Prejudice* (Counter-Currents, 2017), *You Asked for It: Selected Interviews*, vol. 1 (Counter-Currents, 2017), *The White Nationalist Manifesto* (Counter-Currents, 2018), *Toward a New Nationalism* (Counter-Currents, 2019), *Return of the Son of Trevor Lynch's CENSORED Guide to the Movies* (Counter-Currents, 2019), *From Plato to Postmodernism* (Counter-Currents, 2019), *It's Okay to Be White* (Ministry of Truth, 2020); *Graduate School with Heidegger* (Counter-Currents, 2020), and *Trevor Lynch: Part Four of the Trilogy* (Counter-Currents, 2020).

He is editor of *North American New Right*, vol. 1 (Counter-Currents, 2012); *North American New Right*, vol. 2 (Counter-Currents, 2017); *The Alternative Right* (Counter-Currents, 2018); *Dark Right: Batman Viewed from the Right* (with Gregory Hood, Counter-Currents, 2018); Julius Evola, *East and West: Comparative Studies in Pursuit of Tradition* (with Collin Cleary, Counter-Currents, 2018); Collin Cleary, *Summoning the Gods: Essays on Paganism in a God-Forsaken World* (Counter-Currents, 2011); Collin Cleary, *What is a Rune? & Other Essays* (Counter-Currents, 2015); Jonathan Bowden, *Western Civilization Bites Back* (Counter-Currents, 2014); Jonathan Bowden, *Extremists: Studies in Metapolitics* (Counter-Currents, 2017), and many other books.

His writings have been translated into Czech, Danish, Dutch, Estonian, Finnish, French, German, Greek, Hungarian, Norwegian, Polish, Portuguese, Russian, Slovak, Spanish, Swedish, and Ukrainian.

www.ingramcontent.com/pod-product-compliance
Lightning Source LLC
Chambersburg PA
CBHW030853170426
43193CB00009BA/599